THE POWER OF MORE

HOW SMALL STEPS

CAN HELP YOU ACHIEVE

BIG GOALS

THE POWER OF
MORE

MARNIE McBEAN

GREYSTONE BOOKS

D&M PUBLISHERS INC.

Vancouver/Toronto/Berkeley

Greystone Books
An imprint of D&M Publishers Inc.
2323 Quebec Street, Suite 201
Vancouver BC Canada V5T 4S7
www.greystonebooks.com

Cataloguing data available from Library and Archives Canada
ISBN 978-1-926812-64-9 (pbk.)
ISBN 978-1-926812-65-6 (ebook)

Editing by Nancy Flight
Cover design by Peter Cocking and Heather Pringle
Text design by Heather Pringle
Cover photograph © Catherine Farquharson
Printed and bound in Canada by Friesens
Distributed in the U.S. by Publishers Group West

We gratefully acknowledge the financial support of the Canada Council for the Arts,
the British Columbia Arts Council, the Province of British Columbia through the
Book Publishing Tax Credit, and the Government of Canada through the Canada
Book Fund for our publishing activities.

Greystone Books is committed to reducing the consumption of old-growth forests in
the books it publishes. This book is one step towards that goal.

CONTENTS

A collection of photos, videos, and blog entries
related to *The Power of More* can be found at
www.MarnieMcBean.ca.

FOREWORD

'VE known Marnie since I was a teen, when she was training at the Victoria City Rowing Club in my hometown, and I've run into her at two Olympics since. Marnie isn't a multiple gold medallist by chance. As this book describes, she's created a methodology for success that matters. It matters because it sets out the steps needed to get to chosen results. And in Marnie's case, those results are pretty impressive.

Marnie's someone who really exudes confidence. But she's not ego-driven. She just knows the time and effort she has put into determining and reaching her goals and, therefore, the likelihood that she'll be met with success. As a fellow goal setter (and too-short-for-my-chosen-profession professional), I get it. A lot of people have heard the whole "underdog" story about my "improbable rise to the NBA." There's a book about me called *Long Shot*. (I think there's a compliment in there somewhere.) But if you talk to the people closest to me, they didn't have that same "that's impossible" attitude toward my ambitions, and they didn't think I was a nutter or an egomaniac for having them. And I think a lot of my experience is explained by what Marnie writes about here: I had a realistic picture of what would be required to make it to where I wanted to be, and I went about it practically enough that it seemed less outlandish (not *not* outlandish, but less so) to those who knew me best (it's also entirely possible that they just didn't know any better and were just agreeing with me to be kind).

That's a big part of any success: deciding on your aims, making a plan, mapping that plan from start to finish, and, along the way, conceptualizing the realities of what's entailed—whether it's time, resources, personal support, or other factors—in starting out. People often equate being practical with being conservative or unambitious; it doesn't have to be. Because you're taking the time to lay out your path in measurable steps, a practical approach can instill a beautiful confidence that comes from knowing you can actually achieve what you're setting out to do. Sure, fate is always going to jump in and throw you a freak snowstorm or some other mischief, but being attentive to and thoughtful with your planning is paramount to getting where you want to be.

Marnie and I are both athletes, but our life goals aren't limited to sports, and this book isn't about physical feats. "Where you want to be" can mean anything. The tools Marnie sets out here can be adapted to any environment, dream, or hope, which makes this such a useful guidebook. Your own goal can be as spontaneous or inventive as you are, or as simple as "I'm going to keep this pace until I get to that tree" or "I'm going to work on this creative until I have five ideas that I really love." Sure, it can be a game within ourselves, but it's more than a mind trick. It's success at play. And the funny thing about goals is that you're really the only person who knows whether you can achieve them: you know your strengths, your weaknesses, and how committed you are to the work of making your goals happen. Any time you set a goal for yourself, you create the possibility of success; with Marnie's book, you also create a plan to see it through.

What I especially like about Marnie's approach is her direction for the tough spots. Success does not always come easy. As an athlete, I've played at various times in my life with less-than-ideal conditions: flu, a broken nose, a swollen-shut eye, a cut-open face, a sleepless night spent with a toddler (albeit an absolutely adorable one) who woke up at 4 AM and just felt like chatting with her old man for the next three hours, and a degenerative back condition that rarely seems to care about my plans for success. Yet what I need to do performance-wise on a given day doesn't change. Marnie looks at those "bad days" with the same practical approach that shows how to make them work, how to play through with the same positive outlook that comes easily on the good days.

The Power of More, as the title suggests, also has something for those among you who have already accomplished many goals. Marnie's strategies for digging deep to find the next objective and create a plan for it will keep you inspired and driven for years to come. Maybe for Marnie it's making the Olympics in another sport (just kidding—but don't put it past her); maybe for you it's learning a new language or communicating more effectively with your significant other. This book really has something for everyone who is interested in how to get more out of themselves, and more out of life. It teaches you that you can be excited about what comes next, and that you get to dictate so many of the terms for yourself. So read it, and then, as Thoreau said, "go confidently in the direction of your dreams." If knowledge is power, this book really is the Power of More.

STEVE NASH
www.SteveNash.org

ACKNOWLEDGEMENTS

I'VE always enjoyed talking to people about what I've learned from sport, but I never wanted to write a book about my rowing career; I just didn't see the point. From a distance, my sport career was pretty direct: find sport, enter Olympics, win Olympics. Enter Olympics again; win Olympics again. There was no hook or drama to my career as an athlete.

Although it may look as if my success rate at the Olympics was close to 100 per cent, it was actually closer to 50 per cent. I tried out for four Olympic teams and was able to compete in two. I was gutted when I failed to make the 1988 team but came out all aces at the next two, winning a pile of medals at the 1992 and 1996 Games. My fourth attempt was scuttled when I was forced to withdraw just before competition in 2000 because of two ruptured discs in my lower back. My back surgery was successful, but my Olympic racing career ended.

I expected that to be the end to my Olympic journey, but to date I have added another four Olympics to my resumé. When I was an athlete, I could never have imagined being in my current role, mostly because this role never existed—until I created it. I am now a specialist in Olympic athlete preparation and mentoring.

In 2006, when I accepted a volunteer position as athlete services officer for the Winter Olympic team, the Canadian Olympic Committee (COC) helped me to discover my next significant role with our Olympic team, which is no longer just about rowing. I have been the Canadian Olympic Team's athlete mentor for Winter and Summer Games, in all sports, both veteran and rookie, for athletes at the Turin 2006, Beijing 2008, and Vancouver 2010 Games. As soon as the Vancouver Olympics were over, in February 2010, I began working with the Canadian athletes who are preparing for the London 2012 Games.

Working with and supporting the COC, I created a plan designed to help athletes bring the confidence that they have at World Cup and World Championship competitions to the Olympics. We want them to arrive at the Olympic Games with all of their swagger. It is a privilege to work with them; as much as I help them, I learn so much from all of their different sport cultures and transfer these lessons around as I go. I get to work with so many incredible and diverse people who share the same goal: to always do a little more.

After I finished rowing, lessons that support my idea of a career champion came from everywhere—sport, business, and adventure. And the main lesson was that the joy isn't in the *more* that you can get, but in the *more* that you can give and do. I began to see the story I wanted to tell. More—there is a lesson in that. I thought I had a plan, but it wasn't until I sat down with my friend Chris Cook that it really started to take shape. Thanks, Chris; I loved every Thursday chat we had.

AS I WROTE about focus and dedication, I realized that I had to heed my own advice. In the beginning I struggled and needed help to avoid the variety of distractions around me. My thanks to Deanah Shelly and the example she set wading through the intensity and volume of third-year law and articling. It helped me to train my mind the same way I once trained my body. It was a simple lesson: shut the door.

For most of my rowing career, I was partnered with Kathleen Heddle and coached by Al Morrow. From them I learned so much more than just how to be a world and Olympic champion. I continue to be a better friend, partner, and teammate because of them. Canada has never produced a better rower than Kathleen, and I was lucky that she was the port to my starboard. The group that we started with—Brenda Taylor, Kirsten Barnes, Jessica Monroe, Lesley Thompson-Willie, Jenny Walinga, and Julie Jespersen—are the most amazing women; we were joined by so many others: Kelly Mahon, Megan Delehanty, Kay Worthington, and Shannon Crawford to name a few. I was so lucky to learn from them all.

Over the course of my rowing career I learned a tremendous amount from Al Morrow. He was my coach and my mentor. Even as I wrote this book he still taught me something new; I am so glad I asked. To Al; his wife, Julia (where so many of his nuggets of wisdom came from); and their four kids, thank you for sharing so much of your time. Coaching sport is often more than full-time work, for barely part-time pay.

My curiosity came from my parents, and it's a gift that I cherish daily. My mom taught me to go with the flow and to never say no to something just because I didn't know how, and

I'm blessed with my dad's sense of humour and his remarkable ability to figure things out.

Mahalo to my aunt, Sherrill MacLaren, who threw my dream of a book into overdrive. Her guidance and advice turned out to be more than just another fantastic birthday gift, and my dream became a goal.

Derek Covington and Carol Assalian at the Canadian Olympic Committee, you have been very brave! Thank you for giving me the opportunity to be part of the Olympic athlete preparation program—and for giving me the space and freedom to say in my own voice what I wanted to say to the Beijing, Vancouver, and now London Olympic teams. It has been a privilege to be a mentor to Canadian athletes. For a spreadsheet kind of boss, Derek, you let me work fairly organically. Thank you.

To all of the athletes who have let me into their worlds, I am always thankful for your insight and responses to my crazy ideas—I've learned from you more than you know.

I will end here as I do with many of my mentor messages. Think of this as a talking point; you may agree with me, maybe disagree. It may serve as a heads-up or a reminder of the natural ups and downs of believing that you can do more than just go to the Olympics, more than just compete—you can compete at your very *best*.

My goal will be to never add to your stress but to help you wear it well.

Thank you.

INTRODUCTION

Simple Beginnings Can Lead

to Incredible Things

BECAUSE of a chocolate bar commercial that featured rowing and then a movie with Rob Lowe rowing around in jeans, I looked up the Argonaut Rowing Club in the Toronto phone book. I was sixteen and had tried every other sport I'd seen, so why wouldn't I try this one? Hardly an auspicious start to a great sporting career, but from that simple beginning I became North America's most decorated rower, with six world and Olympic gold medals in rowing, four silvers, and two bronzes. My rowing partner, Kathleen Heddle, and I are Canada's most successful Summer Olympians. No one is more surprised by this than I am.

I was recently asked to write an introduction to the section on long-term athlete development (LTAD) for the second edition of the book *Rowing Faster*. LTAD is a hot topic in sport development, and although I was flattered to be asked, I wondered what I could contribute. The goal of LTAD for the governing body of each sport, such as Rowing Canada, Biathlon Canada, or Hockey Canada, is to hone systems and develop programs that support athletes from playground to podium and beyond. Sports are being tasked not just with how to get people involved in recreational and competitive streams but with how to develop and improve their performance as well as encourage a healthy lifestyle. I succeeded despite the system, however, not because of it. I was told that I was a bit too short, I started a bit too late, and my high school didn't have the right sport program. Becoming an Olympic champion did not appear to be in the cards I was dealt. Heck, I watched so much TV and socialized so much that I wonder how I even became an athlete at all!

I took that as the direction for writing my introduction to *Rowing Faster's* LTAD section. I'm sure that there are many athletes, far more talented than myself, who haven't made it through the sport system because too many recruiting programs were set up to develop athletes who were on the "perfect" path. A little struggle to get "there" may be a good thing, but a lot of help and support would be better.

My experience and this story aren't just about struggle, because there are certainly many people who have had to overcome more than I have, but nothing was given to me. I had to figure things out: the realities of systems, teams, and performance; my emotional, physical, and social reactions to these realities; and then how to do more than others, for longer.

I've applied the lessons that helped me achieve my goals in rowing to other endeavours, and I believe that they can be applied to almost any goal out there. Sharing the techniques that I used to become an Olympic champion has helped countless others achieve their goals in sport and life; they have helped me lead a group of teenagers to the summit of Mount Kilimanjaro; aided scores of Olympic and recreational athletes, as well as business associates in countless fields to achieve personal bests; and I used many of them even to write this book. Believing in more has always helped me to simply get the job done.

THE POWER OF MORE

Most people do not consider themselves superheroes. Only the animated superhero character in the movie *Toy Story*, Buzz Lightyear, can say, "To infinity and beyond!" with the full intention of getting there. When faced with a challenging goal, most of the rest of us are often too quick to dismiss ourselves. I have found that it's much easier to achieve big things when they are broken down into little, manageable bits of *more*.

To support a fundraising event for the World Wildlife Fund, I was asked to participate in a race up the stairs to the observation deck of the CN Tower in Toronto. You can see it from a hundred kilometres away, towering above the rest of the city. I'll admit I was a bit concerned; even when I was ready to race at the Olympics I could still get winded after walking a flight of stairs in my house!

From a distance the CN Tower looked like one ginormous step. It was like looking at a superhero's goal, not a mortal's. In reality there are 1,776 steps to get to the top of that tower.

Although that is a lot of steps, I realized that no single step was going to be anything more than just a normal step. The idea of climbing one step after the other made it a normal person's goal. One by one, I ran them all; turned out it wasn't so tough.

Throughout my rowing career there was one concept that resonated with me. The essence of that concept was *more*. Almost every year, Al Morrow, the coach of the Canadian women's rowing team, told us the story of how a Czechoslovak rower, Bob Janousek, and his coxed four won the European Championships (the precursor to the rowing World Championships, which started in 1962). In the battle for first, Janousek thought he was at his limit and wanted to quit, but he kept convincing himself that he could take just ten more strokes. Many of the details of the story varied from year to year, such as where the race was and who they were racing, but the essence of the story always remained the same. If you just do a little more than the competition, you can outlast them and win. Even if you think you are done, you probably aren't; you always have a bit more. I took this lesson to heart and made the word *outlast* a talisman that I used in races to help me keep pushing, even when I wanted to stop. To achieve my goals meant that I would just have to give a little bit more, for a little bit longer than any of my opponents.

Understanding the power of more became central to how I prepared for and attacked every task and challenge I faced. The idea is not to focus on the more you can get or achieve but rather on the more you can do. It's not about *having* more—it's about being able to *do* more. I've learned that I can almost always do more. (I won't deny that the more I can get is always a nice perk!)

I can always prepare a little bit more. There is more to learn, more to listen to, and more ways to try. The more I could have done often becomes clearer with hindsight. But as anyone who has ever tried to cram for a test, prepare for a race, or put together a presentation knows, it's always frustrating to realize that we should have started doing more sooner. Hopefully we learn from each experience and give ourselves more time to prepare next time.

I like to express the power of more with the symbol $\infty+1$: infinity plus one. I took enough math in high school to remember that infinity, by definition, includes all of the possible $+1$s imaginable and I'm aware that $\infty+1$ is redundant. But since I am a normal person, I can't relate to attacking infinitely big goals; that is for superheroes. I do feel quite confident that I can do a lot of little things. If I'm going to reach infinity, it will be by recognizing the importance of each little $+1$ at a time.

NORMAL PEOPLE DOING SPECIAL THINGS

As a mentor, I try to explain that normal people can do special things. I certainly see myself as a normal person with lots of flaws and weaknesses, and so I'm still blown away thinking about the wonderful things that I've been able to do.

When people ask me what it feels like to go to the Olympics or to be an Olympic champion, I still find it hard to answer. Simple words do not do the experience justice. They are never big enough or deep enough; they lack the necessary brilliance and colour. The best answer I can give is to talk about the fireworks at my first Olympics.

In 1992, just before the Barcelona Olympics began, the Canadian Olympic Team gathered in a small stadium called Palau Sant Jordi with all the other national teams from around the world. This fifteen-thousand-seat stadium was simply a holding pen before we would be marched into the Olympic Stadium at Montjuic for the Opening Ceremony of the Olympic Games.

The Opening Ceremony is an extraordinary time for an athlete. Entering an Olympic stadium as your country is announced, with all of the flags and pageantry, is part of almost every athlete's dreams. It means you have been included in a legendary sports tradition. During the ceremony every athlete is filled with confidence and hope, believing it is possible to have the performance of a lifetime, to create the moment each one has dreamt of.

Waiting in the holding tank seemed to take forever! But in the blink of an eye, we were out of the tunnel and the Olympic Stadium opened up in front of us. My heart was pounding. When "CANADA!" was announced, the noise seemed like thunder. We walked around the 400-metre track, and I waved proudly; my smile stretched from ear to ear. Was this a dream? How could I be here? Olympic athletes are special—could I really be one myself? When we finished our loop of the track, we were directed into the centre of the stadium to wait for the athletes from all of the other countries to march in.

There is no way to make a march of athletes from two hundred nations interesting from beginning to end. After waiting for hours, the crowd (and the athletes) got what they'd been waiting for—the end of the line and the home team. If we were received with thunder, then the Spanish team was received with an earthquake. The stadium shook with the noise. The hairs on my arms stood up; it was thrilling.

The Athletes' Oath, the Officials' Oath, a politician saying this, a CEO saying that—to us it all sounded like marbles in someone's mouth. Sound systems in stadiums are designed for people in the seats, not for the players on the field, so it was difficult for us to hear what was being said. It didn't really matter; all we wanted was for the International Olympic Committee president, Juan Antonio Samaranch, to declare the Games open. At last he did.

The flag was raised and the Olympic Cauldron was lit; it was a dramatic ceremony. I still have a blurry photo that I took that shows the archer, who stood just steps from me, and his flaming arrow lighting the cauldron. That image and the scene of the Australian Aboriginal runner Cathy Freeman surrounded by water as she lit the cauldron at the 2000 Sydney Olympics remain favourite memories for me. As I stood there in Barcelona, our Olympic dreams were finally ablaze; it was incredible.

With the Games open, flag raised, flame lit, and the Three Tenors singing, the only thing left that night was the fireworks. I have heard that the organizers of the Barcelona Olympics hoped to evoke the myth of the phoenix, a bird that rises from ashes into something magical. Like a phoenix, the city of Barcelona had recently been revived from industrial ruin and would rise up and give the world the "best Olympic Games ever." The organizers' dream, like that of the athletes, was that the show would be magical. It certainly was to me.

The fireworks display that night was unlike any I'd ever seen, and few have topped it since. A barrage of yellow, red, and gold explosions bombarded our eyes and ears. Describing an astounding display of fireworks is as difficult as explaining what it's like to be an Olympian. There aren't words that are big enough or rich enough to convey the power of that experience. Being an Olympian resonates through you like fireworks;

you feel a deep awe. But being an Olympian does not change who you are; it does not make you more or less than the normal person who believed in a dream.

This book is for anyone who wants to improve—not just the high-performance athletes heading to the Olympics but all normal people trying to do special things. If you have ambition to get better at something, whatever it is, you share a common goal with those of us who believe in improved performance. You want *more*. All endeavours require effort and ambition: work, play, management of finances, renovation, gardening, personal relationships. If you want to improve, you have to want more.

How you set goals, and your accountability and commitment to them, will be decided by how much ambition you choose to apply. In this book, I will discuss how being successful requires embracing two ideas at the same time: pride in what you have already achieved and a constant belief that there is always more to do. Ambitious goal setting, preparation, and action demand that you accept feeling both satisfied and unsatisfied, because no matter how much you do, there is always more that can be done, learned, or tried. Optimally, as you push to improve, you should never quite settle—which makes you a jammed cat. I'll do my best to explain.

1

COMFORTABLY
UNCOMFORTABLE

WHEN I was training and racing as a rower, I constantly wanted to improve. It would have been impossible to become a six-time world and Olympic champion otherwise.

After races I often struggled when people said to me, "You did great." It wasn't that I was disappointed with the result; regardless of whether I had won or lost, I felt a need to do more. Even if I was happy with the result, my first thoughts would be about what I could do better next time. I knew that if I let myself get too comfortable with the status quo, I would cease to get better. To improve at anything, I am convinced that one must constantly believe in more.

In sport or any other task that you are ambitious for, achieving more is what it's all about. It was the rare race where I finished thinking that I'd done everything exactly as I had wanted. Striving for even just a little bit more is how you improve. So while part of me could agree that I "did great," another part of me was already analyzing what had happened and what I should or shouldn't do next time. After a good race I was more comfortable deflecting praise with something like, "Thanks, but my technique was a bit off" or "I was lucky to win today." A big part of my mentoring now is discussing how allowing yourself to be comfortable when you are uncomfortable with your performance or result is the best way to learn and improve.

Sometimes, even though being second or just finishing something is an amazing accomplishment, the intended goal hasn't been achieved (yet!). After a performance—or a race, game, presentation, interview, season, exam, or conversation— it's possible to be proud and disappointed at the same time, and it can be hard to pretend otherwise.

What if I had a personal-best performance but came second? Am I wrong to be both disappointed and happy? Second is really good, but it's also just a whisker from first. How would I receive a compliment then? Recognizing only my happy side rarely felt as if I was being genuine. Knowing that, how do I celebrate a friend who crossed a 10-kilometre finish line for the first time but regretted that he walked part of the way? Do I say, "You did it! Way to go!" or "Better luck next time"? How do you respond to your partner when she has won a new business contract but is miffed that it isn't bigger? The answer is to respectfully say both. In both of these examples, people are both happy and unsatisfied with their performance; one emotion does not have to trump the other. Sometimes enough is never really enough—and that can be a good thing.

To be ambitious for more does not mean that you have to be in a constant state of dissatisfaction or disappointment. Quite the contrary; you have to have a constant belief in yourself and a sense of achievement. This healthy egotism is where confidence comes from. But when a soccer player makes the team's starting lineup for the first time or a runner completes the whole 10 kilometres, it is up to the performer to know if that was the last step or simply the next step toward the goal. The first goal can be seamlessly replaced with another: run faster, score the winning goal, or win by a bigger margin. Sometimes this raising of the bar can surprise even ourselves; we didn't know we wanted to take the next step until it became available to us.

EMBRACING DUALITY

The trick for improved performance is to accept the duality of being proud/satisfied and unsettled/unsatisfied—being able to see and accept what you did do and what you didn't. Understanding this allowed me to excel as a competitor, and now it is where my mentoring always starts. Embracing performers' perspectives on *their* ambition, regardless of their quest—elite sport, recreational activity, business, or hobby—is the key to understanding what drives them forward. It is a mistake to underestimate or discount an ambitious desire for more.

As a young up-and-comer with the Canadian national rowing team, when I didn't make the 1988 Olympic team, I hated hearing well-meaning statements like "You are young," "Your career has just started," and "You'll have lots of success soon enough." They may have been true, but they were out of sync with my ambitions—the *more* that I felt and wanted now.

Often friends and family (parents might be the worst) are not great at this understanding. They see only what was achieved and want you to look past what you feel you missed or failed in. Although this may be good advice, if the performer has ambition to become better in the future, it's not likely to be possible. Ambition to improve *requires* the performer to remember and focus on what wasn't done—this is how you learn and ensure that more will be achieved in the future.

THE JAMMED CAT THEORY

When people are both proud of what they did do and disappointed in what they didn't do, they are in an optimal state for learning and improvement. This constant desire for more, satisfied yet unsatisfied, led me to develop my jammed cat theory of performance.

If you drop a cat, it supposedly always lands on its feet. But if a piece of toast with jam on it falls from your hands, it always seems to land jam-side down. So if you were to "jam" the back of a cat and drop it, it should never land. It would hover just above the ground, constantly rotating—flipping from feet to jam to feet to jam.

I developed this theory in 2008, when I was in Beijing in a support role with the Canadian Olympic Team. I went by many titles—athlete service officer, peer performance mentor, Olympic champion, lounge manager—but sometimes I felt that mascot was the most apt descriptor. The Canadian Olympic Committee (coc) had asked me to help Canadian athletes feel comfortable in the Olympic environment. Together the coc and I had developed a program to help athletes bring the assuredness they have at the World Cup (an international series of competitions) and the World Championships to the Olympics. The Olympic Games are outside of their normal routine; they are massive multi-sport environments that thrust athletes into a bigger and brighter spotlight than they've experienced anywhere else. We wanted them to arrive with swagger.

For the eleven thousand athletes at the Beijing Summer Olympics, there were only 302 events in which to win a medal. Even though most may have good to great performances, more athletes leave Olympic Games disappointed with their result than leave happy; often they want to have done more. Although not everyone goes to the Olympics with a medal as a realistic goal, that is probably every Olympic athlete's dream goal. I should add that even the medallists aren't completely happy with their performance. Often high-performance athletes are trained to see and work on what they didn't accomplish, and so they don't tend to see anything positive in what they have done.

As the athlete mentor to the Canadian Olympic Team, I needed a tool to start a conversation with our athletes. Some may have had another competition within days, others not until the next season, but it was important to help them make sense of all of their emotions so that they could move on. I don't know how I connected back to a crazy discussion that I'd had more than fifteen years earlier to find this tool, but I did. At the University of Western Ontario I'd been working evenings at the Ceeps tavern, getting up early for 6 AM rowing practices and trying to keep my academic average up in my honours kinesiology program. An exhausted brain can come up with some pretty wild stuff, and mine came up with the jammed cat.

In a cafeteria between classes, a friend had dropped her toast with jam on it, and it landed jam-side down. Doesn't it always? Somehow the conversation progressed from this dropped piece of toast to the fact that if a cat is dropped, it always manages to land on its feet. What if we put the two together? Which side would win? The cat or the jam? The jammed cat, we decided, would never land, as it perpetually rotated from feet to jam to feet to jam.

That crazy concept came back to me late one evening at the Beijing Olympics. Walking through the Olympic Village, I met up with an athlete who was obviously quite sad. I had never met her before, but we were wearing the same Canadian Olympic uniform—we were teammates—so I reached out and said hello. This was her first Olympic competition, and after winning her first judo match she had lost the next two and was knocked out of the competition. "I'm really disappointed," she told me. They were not the kind of bouts that she should have lost. She had hoped to finish at least seventh, but she had finished ninth.

As she explained how her sport worked and the ambition and expectations that she'd had coming into her first Olympics, it was easy to see how conflicted she was by her emotions. With eyes red from crying, she also told me she was really happy to have qualified for the Olympics, but she had hoped for more. As a mentor, I had to help her learn from this experience so that she could improve for the next. I knew I should say something, but I wasn't sure what.

To make her smile, I told her about the jammed cat theory and connected her to it. I didn't try to placate or patronize her. Her Olympics were over, and she felt neither satisfied with the result nor done with her sport. She wanted more. I felt it was important to encourage her to embrace being both satisfied and unsatisfied. I acknowledged her disappointment but said that she didn't have to let go of being proud. Hearing that an Olympic champion understood her, she said, was very comforting.

I realized that this jammed cat idea, embracing duality, could apply to performers all around me. The cat represents a goal, and the jam the ambition for more. Whether you choose to apply ambition to a particular task is up to each individual. If you remove your ambition from a goal, because you have completed it or decided it is time to move on to something new, then, no longer driven to reach improved performance, that cat does not spin; it simply lands. You don't have to be ambitiously driven in all areas of your life. For some things you do, you can be satisfied with the organic pace at which you learn, move, and achieve. But as soon as ambition becomes involved, things change; being just comfortable is not an option.

As you become more ambitious, you become increasingly proactive and reach out for more—faster. If you want to change and improve the performance of your task, you will choose to jam your cat. Being ambitious doesn't require constant dissatisfaction with everything or negative, self-deprecating thoughts. It simply exists because you want more and—what may be more important—you believe in more.

It took me a long time to realize it, but a jammed cat isn't always disappointed in the result; you don't have to lose to still want more. Realizing that this jammed cat idea applied to the winners as well was what made me recognize that being ambitious is about always wanting to do more as much as, if not more than, simply wanting to win. Listening to the Canadian speed skater Christine Nesbitt after she won an Olympic gold medal reminded me that just because you win, it doesn't mean you didn't still want a bit more.

In 2010, Christine was the favourite in the 1,000-metre long-track speed skating event. Since she had won four World Cup races in that event that season, it wasn't surprising when she claimed the Olympic gold medal as well. What was surprising to many was how critical she remained of herself after achieving her goal. After the race, when she showed me her medal, she told me it was an ugly race and that she was kind of disappointed with it. With only 0.02 seconds as her margin of victory, she felt it was only luck that had let her win. Holding her medal and smiling, she said to the media, "I've skated a lot better 1,000s this year, so it's hard for me not to be critical because that's how I've improved."

Happy with the result but not satisfied with her performance, Christine was another example of a jammed cat. She absolutely believed that there was more out there—more to learn, more strength to acquire, more speed to tap into. Turns out she was right; there was. Since the Vancouver Olympics she has completely dominated the 1,000-metre event and many other distances too.

The quantity and quality of the more that you demand will ramp up with your ability to achieve it. I couldn't demand Olympic levels of more when I was at a learn-to-row level; I had to work up to it. Your immediate demand for more must fit not only the size of the goal but your current ability to perform it. Otherwise it's impossible to achieve any duality; you will be either completely satisfied or completely unsatisfied. To be able to reach your ultimate goals, you must be patiently impatient.

Anxiety occurs when there is a mismatch between the size of your goal and your desire to achieve more while doing it. Trying to perform a very complex task with little to no thought for more, or trying to do something very basic with a tremendous amount of desire for more, often leaves the performer with little ability to find any satisfaction. In both situations you end up feeling as if you just couldn't do enough.

In the constant push for more, if you are never happy with any performance, then you are just never happy. But if you can't embrace the duality of being both satisfied and a little unsatisfied, you can run the risk of over-excusing yourself for a poor performance. If you don't want more, you don't try for more—and, even more dangerously for performance, you are okay with less. "Today's result was poor, but it doesn't matter." Or "I didn't really feel like going for it." Or "The conditions were in everyone else's favour, so I didn't bother." If you don't see the need to try (try harder or try more), then in the presence of a challenge, it's easy not to.

There is an end point to applying your ambition and wanting more. The need to embrace duality exists only in situations where you care about improved performance. For the cat to land, without being constantly spun off its feet by a desire for more, simply requires that you be content, hopefully happy, with the status quo. If you have achieved your goal, you don't want to do it any longer, or it's just time to move on, then, in the absence of ambition, reaching for more just isn't important anymore. Congratulations, you're done. *Che sarà sarà.*

But often the end of one goal is just the beginning of another. If you still see new possibilities, then it is very likely that you won't be completely content or finished. You are of two minds: proud of what you have done *and* unhappy about what you haven't. You feel a passionate self-inflicted desire to push constantly for more.

This perpetual push for more is the ideal state not only for an elite athlete but also for all who strive for excellence in their performance. The casual runner who wants to run the whole way in a 10-kilometre race, a club soccer player who wants to earn a spot on the team's starting line, a sales manager trying to improve sales, and a gardener who wants an amazing-looking garden for a Labour Day party are all people who embrace a duality in their performance. They all follow a common pattern to improving performance: they will be feeling the power of more.

2

GOAL SETTING:

It All Starts Here

I **HAD** achieved a dream. A gold medal was placed around my neck and then another around my teammate Kathleen's. We had just won at the Olympics. Standing on the podium and hearing my national anthem had become one of my goals years before. Seconds later, things weren't going entirely as I'd envisioned them: was I really getting the words to our anthem wrong? I was reminded that when it comes to goal setting, although you might have a very clear picture in mind of what you want to achieve, getting there will almost never be exactly as you planned.

Seven hundred and fifty metres into the Olympic final of the women's pair rowing event at the 1992 Barcelona Olympics, we were ahead. The whole race, 2,000 metres, should take only about seven minutes, and after three minutes we were already winning. I was going to be wearing a medal and singing our anthem at the Olympics—OMG.

For two years the Germans and the Americans had been nipping at our heels, and the French and the British thought they had a chance to win too. The race profile that Kathleen Heddle and I had established in this event had been very consistent. So far, in all of our races, if we were in the lead after the first 1,000 metres, no one had been able to pass us in the second 1,000 metres.

Once, the Germans had beaten us, but we had made two mistakes—one technical at the beginning of the race and one tactical at the end. There was no guarantee that we wouldn't make the same technical error, but we were determined not to make the tactical error again. The Americans had *almost* beaten us in a race earlier that year, but almost doesn't get you a gold medal. Their tactic had been to front-load all of their energy into the start and the first quarter of the race. They gave anything and everything early in the race to try to finally beat us. Spending energy in a race is no different from spending money from your savings account. You have only so much of it, so you have to budget. The U.S. team did in fact jump out to an early lead, and then they could only hope to have enough energy left to stay ahead to the end of the race. On that day, Kathleen and I learned just how powerful our second 1,000 metres in a race could be. When we made our usual attack at the 1,000-metre mark, we flew. All the American crew could do was watch us go by; they had no energy left to respond to us.

With the confidence that we could win from the back of the pack if we had to, being out in the front in this race, the Olympic final, was a rush. Physically what we were doing was extremely hard, but... this was amazing! I was achieving my goal!

During a race, my eyes focus mostly on Kathleen's back. I sit behind her and need to stay in sync and keep my power application—my rhythm—matched to hers. Between the two of us, I had the speaking role in our boat and was responsible for talking us through our race plan. And as always, at 750 metres, I was supposed to say, "Quick, explosive legs. Let's drive them down. Let's go!" But who can say all that when her heart rate is at 205 beats per minute? So as always, "Legs" it was. Usually I'm very focussed on our task during a race, but in this particular one, my mind started to wander.

In rowing, since rowers sit facing backwards, being in the lead provides an extra advantage. Being at the front of the pack means you get to watch the crews that are chasing you, allowing you to see and respond when an opponent makes an attack. I was watching the other five boats—Germany, France, USA, Great Britain, and Bulgaria—and I didn't think they had a chance to catch us. We were coming up to the 1,000-metre mark and our speed was about as fast as it had ever been. We were winning; we were winning the Olympic final! In my mind's eye I could almost see the medal that was waiting for us. That sort of in-race arrogance and lack of focus can lead to problems, including the same type of technical mistake that had let the Germans beat us previously.

TASK! Our coach, Al Morrow, had repeatedly said that the way to accomplish our goal was to focus on the task. The image of the word smacked me back to the reality at hand. The medals were still up for grabs—we hadn't finished the race yet—I had more to do. My task wasn't to think about how shiny and heavy the medal was going to be around my neck as

I sang the anthem but to put my oars in the water and pull as hard as I could, again and again. Thankfully, focussing on my task brought me back; we had worked way too hard to ruin it all by celebrating before we had finished.

With about 300 metres to go, our lead was solid. I could see that three boats—the Germans, the Americans, and the French—were fighting to get into the silver and bronze positions. I knew they would do anything to avoid finishing fourth. In a situation like that, when a race is close or the consequences are great, people can search deep within themselves for that little bit more. I've seen boats go from first to fourth not because they went more slowly, but because they failed to recognize that everyone else was applying a bit more effort. I pointed out this battle for medals to Kathleen and quickly added a new call to our race plan: "We—have—to—go—NOW!"

It worked. Not only did we stay in the lead but we also crossed the finish line with an Olympic-best time for our event. At that moment, I didn't want to move, let alone row to the podium dock. I had finally earned the right to envision wearing my medal and singing the Canadian anthem, but all I could do was slump over my oar and gasp for air. I may have been dreaming of winning a medal, but I had been preparing for my task, to row well and win a race. Which was exactly what we did.

What was our first emotion upon crossing the finish line? Relief—relief that we hadn't screwed up. We had rowed the race we'd trained for. With hardly time to catch our breath, we were directed to the podium dock.

We got out of the boat and I looked up. The Canadian fans, who included my parents and brother, were going wild! It was like a dream; they were laughing, crying, and waving flags like crazy. Kathleen and I had won races before, so the routine was familiar to me: row to dock, climb out of boat, hug Kathleen, shake hands with our competitors, stand in line, and, after the trumpet fanfare, be presented with our medals. But this one was different. Big, heavy Olympic medals now hung around our necks; our anthem was about to be played. At rowing World Championships, national anthems are not played for medal ceremonies, so for me, this would be a first. I think that is why singing the anthem was such an important part of my dream and goal setting.

The reason I got into rowing has a lot to do with TV. I had seen the 1984 Olympics in Los Angeles, and my dream was to go to the Olympics for the party. I thought the Closing Ceremony looked like a blast. Not long after, I saw the movie *Oxford Blues* and then that chocolate bar commercial with rowing in it. It's not a stretch to say that TV led me to learn to row.

When I'd seen the Olympics on TV, I really liked it when the athletes sang at their medal ceremonies. I thought it made them look so much more involved. It became my dream that I would sing like that. About a year earlier I'd bought a tape with different versions of "O Canada" for my car. I wanted to be really comfortable with the Canadian anthem so that it would come naturally to me; I guess I trained for it too!

Standing on the podium with our gold medals, when "O Canada" began, I was ready to sing. Both Kathleen and I sang, but about halfway in, I was struck by a horrible realization: I was getting the words wrong. So was Kathleen. We stopped and listened to the music; what was going on?

To everyone watching TV, it must have looked as if I didn't know the words to my own anthem. It turned out that the International Olympic Committee had shortened national anthems down to forty-five seconds to fit into a commercial break. A whole chunk of "O Canada" had been removed, but no one had warned us. There I was on the Olympic podium, receiving a gold medal, with my anthem playing, and I was getting the words wrong. My Olympic dream image was being ruined.

When I could figure out where we were in the song, I joined in again. With only about ten seconds left, it finally sank in: this was the medal ceremony at the Olympic Games. I had a gold medal around my neck, our flag was being raised, and our anthem was being played because we had earned it. We had rowed the race we wanted. Singing didn't seem so important anymore; I stopped and cried.

Within the goal-setting process, there are important-to-haves and nice-to-haves. Although singing the anthem was the cherry on top of the sundae, at that moment, I clearly understood that rowing a great race was the ice cream and the chocolate sauce. Everything else—the flag, the anthem, and even the medal—were just nice-to-haves, but it turned out they weren't my real goal at all.

Drill down and know what is really important. I was really lucky to learn this lesson after I had achieved my first big goal and to learn it early in my career. Too often, I've seen people get distracted by what they think is important before they achieve their goal. Athletes, politicians, doctors, students— you name it, they can all fall into the same trap of counting their chickens (or dollars!) before they hatch, believing their own press before they've actually crossed the finish line. They start wanting to be treated like career champions when really they aren't yet more than flashes in the pan. Usually, once you actually establish yourself as a career champion, being treated like one by others isn't so important to you.

TURNING DREAMS INTO GOALS

Dreams and goals are not the same. Dreams are the seed from which all goals arise; they are the fantasy images that we picture for ourselves. Dreams are extremely personal in both scale and type. A big, seemingly impossible dream for one person may be part of someone else's everyday life. One person may dream of overcoming a fear of flying, whereas another person may fly all the time without ever being afraid.

The possibilities for our dreams are endless. They can be physical (complete a triathlon), financial (save a little bit each week), personal (dress nicely), or spiritual (laugh regularly). Whatever it is that you decide is important can be your dream. Whether your dream requires an antagonist or not, whether it belongs to you alone or is shared by a group, or whether it was suggested to you by someone else doesn't make a difference. How important each of your dreams is to you is a personal decision—there is no right or wrong.

Dreams can be wonderful, but they have little depth. They present themselves to us as simple images in our minds—as pictures of unique moments in time. When you close your eyes, how do your dreams present themselves to you? What do your pictures look like? What do they mean to you? It doesn't matter whether your dream is about how you see yourself or about how others see you. What matters is that it is yours and that it has some significance to you.

An athlete's dream might be to stand on the podium, arms high, waving the champion's bouquet, with a large gold medal hanging from her neck. A hockey player might see himself kissing the Stanley Cup and then holding it above his head. A medical student might imagine herself in a high-tech operating room performing complicated surgery while being observed and admired by colleagues. Some people might see themselves in front of a large house, surrounded by happy kids and grandkids. Maybe your dream image is of yourself sitting in a certain kind of car or going on a ski vacation or breaking through the finish tape of a triathlon.

As single images they are all very appealing, but in this dream form, lacking any plan, they have no depth and there is no mechanism to achieve them. They are isolated future moments with no connection to where you stand today. A dream has no path—that's why it's just a dream.

It's impossible to know why we choose to turn some dreams into goals and not others; everyone's goals are different. To create a goal, you must somehow connect the present moment to a future moment that appeals to you. You do this by envisioning a collection of images that reveal (or begin to reveal) the work and effort that will take you to that future moment. These images show the many steps in your goal-setting plan. The more images in the plan, the more detailed your goal setting is and the more real the goal becomes. You can achieve your goal by following the goal-setting path. Then it's no longer just a dream; it's a goal.

CHOOSING YOUR GOAL

I've never been to Mount Everest, but I've heard stories from people who have. I've heard from climbers whose experiences of reaching the 29,000-foot summit included frostbite, agony, danger, and the death of their guides. As you would expect, these people are extraordinarily proud of their accomplishment. That is one goal that holds zero appeal for me. It has never been my dream.

I've also heard from people who have been to base camp at 19,000 feet on Mount Everest. They are just as proud of their achievement as those who have reached the summit. In fact, I once went to hear two men speaking about their journey up Mount Everest. They were so passionate about the effort and the struggle that when the story of their journey concluded at base camp, I was shocked. Where was the rest of the story? For them, I learned, that was their story. Their idea of more had pushed them to get to base camp. That was their final photo, not the summit. This in no way diminishes the value of their goal and journey. We all need to choose and believe in the goals that are right for us. The scale of someone else's goal does not diminish or inflate our own.

I tend to aim high. My mom always used to quote Robert Browning to me: "A man's reach should exceed his grasp, or what's a heaven for?" For an athlete who was barely learning her sport to dream about the Olympics, I may well have been reaching beyond my grasp, but why impose limits on a dream or a goal? What's wrong with at least exploring the idea and trying? It's often people without big dreams and goals of their own who tend to pull others down before they even start. Why would someone discourage a corporate intern from dreaming about running the company one day or hold back a young girl who loves to sing and has plans to be the next Katy Perry? You have to start somewhere.

No one should judge what does or doesn't scare you. Knowing whether base camp is your final destination or just one of many images on the way to the summit is what's important. Remember, there is no courage without fear, so be prepared to accept a little fear with some of your goal setting. This fear isn't the monster-in-the-closet variety, it's more fear of failure, which, depending on how badly you wanted the goal and how complex the path to achieve it is, can range from devastation to slight disappointment.

That said, not all of your goals should be really scary. Some goals need only push you enough so you remain interested in them. The risk of success or failure for these goals is being slightly happy or slightly disappointed. Some easy successes are necessary, but too easy is just so... beige.

I believe we all should have some goals that scare us. It's not often that you see people rejoicing after achieving an easy target. There is no joy in overachieving on a mediocre goal, and we'll never be qualified to know our own limits until we try—and I mean *really* try.

I enjoy watching runners in the Goodlife Fitness Toronto Marathon when they go by my house, which is located in the first third of the race. As the front-runners fly by, they look relaxed, almost bored. I imagine they are focussed on staying relaxed and maintaining their pace, wondering if they will finish a minute or two faster or slower than their goal. After 15 kilometres of the 42-kilometre race, these competitors rarely have friends and family out to cheer them on. Why? Because for them, the scale of fear or risk is very small early in the race; completing the whole distance is not their goal— a specific time is. Their friends and family will be closer to the finish, where they can encourage the runners to maintain their pace and thus achieve their goals.

I sip my coffee and cheer as the runners continue to stream by. Soon I notice a shift in the expressions on the runners' faces. The sleek bodies and relaxed faces of the front-runners are replaced by normal and even soft physiques, and faces that show stress and possibly a bit of fear. It is obvious that some of these runners are wondering if they will make it to the finish;

mentally or physically some of them are struggling already. I admire this group so much. They have set goals they are not sure they can achieve, but they are going for it anyway. Their friends and family support them at many points along the course and encourage them just to keep moving.

At the finish the front-runners cross the line, check their time, and, even though they are completely spent, often walk away with barely a hitch in their step. A time that is one or two minutes (or even seconds!) faster or slower than their goal would be extremely significant to them. The pace they set for themselves is extremely demanding and can be scary, but they knew they'd get to the finish; it was a question of how fast.

After this high-performance group, a large cohort of runners come through who were also confident that they would finish. Based on the commitment they put into their training, they may have been hoping for a specific time goal, but the run itself is the ultimate goal. They will be slightly happy or slightly disappointed with their time, but because their goal is broad, and relatively doable, they cross the line content; it has been a good run.

Six, seven, or even eight hours into the race, when people are barely making it to the end—that's when the emotional celebrations take place. Even as it's obvious that the runners are mentally and physically suffering, you can see the moment they realize that they have done something really hard, something they had sincerely doubted they could do. But they tried anyway and that is what they celebrate. They are beaming with pride; their exhausted smiles stretch from ear to ear.

This may be more of a gut feeling than a fact, but it seems that children, far more than adults, are willing to accept some risk and try new things. When do people start to reject ventures that are unknown to them because they seem impossibly hard? How many times have you avoided trying something because you thought it would be too hard, even though you'd never tried it? Kids are so willing to explore, be curious, and try.

Too often we make the mistake of seeing only what we can do today while imagining the demands of the goal in the future. In the absence of a chain of images connecting now to then, we forget to create a doable path and doubt our ability to bridge that gap. When we see examples of success, we tend to compare ourselves with those established successful role models, asking, "Am I like that person?" The question should be, "Could I be like that person?"

PASSION GOALS VERSUS WANT GOALS

On good and great days, when we are challenged, we will almost always try. Here the difference between want and passion goals stands out. If the goal is a passion goal, we try because all we want is more. We attend classes and take clinics; we read and learn and do more. We will make the effort to fill in the space between our "now" image and our "future" image. What others see as a gamble we see as a calculated risk with odds we believe we can beat. With a passion goal, even on our bad days we are more than likely to try for more.

But just because you can do something doesn't mean that you should. Goal setting isn't just about doing what you can do. For big and long-term goals, you have to consider how much you want to do it. There is a commitment of time and effort in every goal. It's always better if you feel you chose to be challenged instead of being stuck with the challenge; this is the difference between choice and sacrifice.

Some goals are way too hard or take up too much time for you to do them just because you can. When Brett Farve, the quarterback of the National Football League's Green Bay

Packers, announced that he wanted to retire, he said that he still wanted to play the game; he just didn't want to practise anymore. To me this was the perfect reason to retire. (He didn't stay retired, but that's another story.) He knew he could still play football, but his desire to be committed to everything else that was required was gone. It was no longer his passion.

If you've set yourself a big goal, or a long-term one, sooner or later it's going to get difficult. There will be mental, physical, and emotional challenges every step of the way. If the goal is a passion goal, something you need to do, then it doesn't matter what the challenge is: you will remain hungry to try. Your ambition and drive will continue to push you to learn and do more. Your passion won't allow you to be content with your current status.

Some goals need a lot of energy and ambition, others just a little. A passion goal can sometimes fade into something you just want, or maybe you realize it's more someone else's goal than your own. Either way, the natural evolution for many goals is that at some point you will run out of the ambition needed to keep you spinning for more. When your goal becomes something you barely even want to do, it is easy to notice everything you are missing out on—the sacrifices. It's more likely to feel like a burden.

This is another reason why it is so important, when setting goals, that you be clear *why* you are (re)setting, and accepting, a goal. Is it really your goal? Are you prepared to embrace it as your goal? Even easy goals require some ambition and effort, and that's going to have to be applied by you. It's not likely that you'll know all of the details at the outset, but it's important to have some idea of what you are getting yourself into. If you willingly choose to go forward, then the challenges that will follow will be easier to embrace. In the absence of choice, when challenges pile up, you can become bitter about all that you aren't doing—your sacrifices—instead of being engaged by the effort and rewards of what you have chosen to do.

If the goal is simply something you want, then your level of confidence plays a bigger role. Because confidence naturally waxes and wanes, when you are setting your goal, you need to develop a specific vision about what is important to you. When your level of confidence is low, you tend to lose some of your ambition. You then question how hard a bit more might be rather than paying attention to how much you want to achieve your goal. The thought of the effort blocks the connection to the goal. Are you willing to risk disappointment or failure? If you know how much you want to achieve the goal, and even why you want it, you may be willing to give a bit more.

People often use past failures to put limits on themselves. But failing once does not mean failing forever. Anything worthwhile is likely going to be hard. Your previous experiences should be used as a tool to help you understand the challenges you now face, not as a weapon to discourage you from trying.

In the Vancouver Olympic hockey tournament, Sidney Crosby took twenty-eight shots and scored four times.

First game:	3 shots	no goals
Second game:	6 shots	1 goal
Third game:	3 shots	1 goal
Fourth game:	5 shots	1 goal
Fifth game:	4 shots	no goals
Sixth game:	3 shots	no goals

In the seventh and final game, he took four shots and scored the game winner for the Olympic gold medal. His average experience of scoring only once in seven attempts didn't discourage him from shooting; he expected scoring to be hard, so missing simply encouraged him to try some more.

The experience of misses and failures collects in us, and unfortunately we tend to remember all of them far more clearly than we do our successes. This affects our level of confidence, and as we approach new things, we evaluate our next steps based on the emotional toll our previous failures have taken. As a result, we often hesitate and then bail on the idea. This is the exact moment when a desire for more can have the maximum benefit. If you have clearly defined your goal and have filled in all the big gaps with little incremental steps of more, reaching that goal becomes a lot less scary—and more likely.

This is where mentors can be so helpful. Sometimes you are close to accomplishing a task but are missing the key action that can connect you to the next step. As part of her TV show, *Fearless in the Kitchen,* the host and professional chef Christine Cushing is tasked with teaching a terrible cook how to be capable in the kitchen. I was involved in an episode where the guest struggled to make anything palatable. Despite her repeated efforts, her family had given up on her. Even her attempts to make Kraft Dinner were unsuccessful. Following what she believed to be the directions, she had cooked the noodles in four cups of water and added the butter and the packet of cheese powder. She couldn't understand why her macaroni and cheese looked more like a soup. She even added a second packet of the cheese powder to thicken it up. Her try-and-try-again approach wasn't working until her mentor, Christine, pointed out a few steps she was missing— most notably, draining off the water!

More commonly, it might take just a two-minute conversation for one co-worker to point out to another a simple keyboard shortcut in Word or Excel that makes a complicated task simple. The exchange of ideas, tactics, and techniques with peers and mentors coupled with a desire to try again is the most effective way to keep us focussed on the way forward instead of on our misses in the past.

GOALS UNLIMITED

Setting goals that challenge you is tricky because it involves so much more than being brave: you have to be creative. Many goal-setting paths are similar, but none are identical; we will all have our own unique crosses to bear. Sometimes you have to envision yourself doing something faster or more efficiently, even if few people, if any, have shown the way. You have to be open to change and growth, and you must believe that what you think is impossible might be possible after all.

Breaking the four-minute mile was once considered an impossible feat. In the 1940s, pundits around the world said it was beyond human capacity to run that fast. Some went so far as to predict that it would be fatal. Even so, after a disappointing loss at the 1952 Olympics, the British athlete Roger Bannister set a goal to break the four-minute mile.

In 1954, at a track in Oxford, England, Bannister won a race in a time of 3 minutes, 59.4 seconds; this feat was later commemorated in the movie *Chariots of Fire*. Bannister did the "impossible" but just forty-six days later, the Australian runner John Landy broke that record. By the end of 1957, sixteen runners had broken the four-minute barrier. Apparently a sub-four-minute mile was neither impossible nor fatal!

Very early in my training, I had a teammate who was doing a master's degree in sport psychology. Tragically, a drunk driver killed her while she was out for a morning run, but her memory and her work have stayed with me. As I remember it, Mary Lynn had asked thirty people to be part of her study. All of them were competitive rowers. She asked them to do a six-minute test on a rowing machine and instructed them all to prepare for, and chase, their personal-best (PB) score, as measured in revolutions. All of the information during the test would come to them via the tester, not directly from the machine.

The first group of ten were told their stroke rate (number of strokes per minute) at each fifteen-second and forty-five-second interval. At each thirty-second and sixty-second interval they were told their pace, which on this particular machine was measured in revolutions per minute. This was Mary Lynn's control group. As expected, they scored very close to their personal bests.

When the second group of ten did the test, the same information was given—with the exception of a little lie. The athletes were told their stroke rate accurately, but they were also told that their pace was faster than it actually was. The tester added 10 revolutions to each interval marker score; for instance, if the rower pulled 300 revolutions in thirty seconds, she was told she'd done 310. Thus, the rowers in this group were led to believe that they were about to make a significant improvement in their PBs. The results of this group were quite different from the first group's. The final score for these rowers was significantly below their personal bests. The size of their potential improvement had scared them into backing off so that they could be sure they would complete the test. Missing their personal bests by 100 to 200 revolutions showed that they had basically chickened out.

The third group received the opposite lie. They were told they were rowing more slowly than they actually were.

Although they were led to believe that they were about to have a significantly bad test, the results from this group were exceptional. The size of their potential dip in score and the accompanying frustration or perhaps embarrassment pushed them to step up their performance. Each rower established a new PB, some by 200 revolutions, a significant margin.

Since everyone had been asked to try to achieve a new benchmark, the rowers in all three groups should have gone as hard as they could. Those in the first (control) group, whose minds and bodies were in sync, did just that. Those in the second group allowed themselves to doubt their physical ability, regardless of what they felt. As they eased back from the "inflated" high pace, what became a relaxed pace should have felt easy and allowed them to go harder. Instead, they settled into what their minds told them they *should* do as opposed to what their bodies felt they *could* do. Those in the third group were just the opposite. They pushed their bodies to achieve the pace they thought they should be able to maintain, even though it would have felt like so much more. What they achieved was more than they had previously thought themselves capable of.

In both situations it was the mind, not the body's physical abilities, that dictated the result. What Mary Lynn was able to show, and what has always resonated with me, was how much our minds can limit—or propel—us.

A few years later, I was struggling to row 2,000 metres in less than seven minutes on a rowing machine. On a number of occasions I could get very close to breaking that seven-minute mark, but I seemed to be stuck. The significance of Mary Lynn's study came back to me. The type of rowing ergometer I was using gave me constant direct information about my pace and rate. My mind was being given way more information than I'd get when I raced on the water, where I would go almost completely on "feel." One day I decided to mimic this lack of information on the erg; I would let my body perform without all of the mental calculations. For my next test, I blocked the screen's information and let my body go as hard as it could. Almost easily, I broke through seven minutes—not just by a little, but by a lot! I was surprised at how much my brain had been limiting me. The information that was supposed to be helping me make good pacing decisions had actually been holding me back.

No matter how much you learn and how much experience you gain, you will never be qualified to know what your own limits are. You often have a little bit more inside you than you allow yourself to believe. If you remove your self-limiting thoughts, you will become far more likely to embrace big goals and then, as you accomplish them, to become more confident in adjusting and expanding them.

"I'M NOT GOING TO GET BEAT BY GOOFY"

Dreams are sometimes born when we see someone else achieving something we admire. We think, "How cool it would be if that were me!" We then elevate that person to be some sort of hero who has achieved greatness and so must be a great person. We see all of that person's strengths. In contrast, we look at ourselves and see all of our weaknesses—our frailties, our doubts, our bad habits. We fail to recognize that our hero might have some of these same doubts and weaknesses.

I first made the national rowing team at the junior (eighteen and under) level. I knew very little about the history of rowing or which countries were the power nations. East

Germany, Romania, and the Soviet Union were the only nations that stood on the podium in women's rowing. They had been pretty much unbeatable. But I didn't know that.

When I arrived with the rest of the very green Canadian team at the Junior World Championships, we found our boat, a pair, on a rack right underneath the Romanian pair. I had to admit that Romania sounded pretty exotic to me; I was maybe a bit intimidated. When I saw a girl preparing to row that boat, I assumed she was my competitor. I was excited to be meeting my competition and thought I'd say hello. Since I didn't speak Romanian, I just gave her one of our Rowing Canada pins. She got very excited—too excited, I thought—practically jumping up and down. I watched her tell her coach about this simple pin I had given her. I thought she was behaving pretty goofily, and I said to myself, "This girl isn't so exotic. She's kinda goofy, like me. I'm not going to get beat by Goofy." And we didn't. Canada came in third. Romania was fourth.

When I returned to Canada, the senior team was blown away that we had defeated one of the "super-nations"; they thought we had done something extraordinary. I didn't understand what the big deal was. I had unexpectedly taught myself an important lesson. The Romanian rower was just a girl, no different from me. I had unwittingly evened the playing field and made the event about ordinary people. For sure we were trying to do something hard, but I didn't have to take down a superpower to do it. Normal people like me can do special things.

Your goal setting should take into account current stats and information, but it shouldn't be limited by them. Statistics aren't just goals for or against, shooting percentages, or size. Stats can be generated from very objective criteria, like your education, career level, and pay status, or from subjective criteria like artistic taste, general fitness, or emotional balance. Just because you didn't go to the "best" school or you're not at the biggest firm or you don't match the perfect stereotype doesn't mean you can't be the exception to the rule. Although there is value in knowing what the stats are, sometimes ignoring information and statistics is the only way to move forward.

When the Canadian women's hockey team went to the 2002 Winter Olympics in Salt Lake City, Utah, they were zero for eight in their previous games against the United States. A win was improbable, but that didn't stop the Canadians from believing that they could eventually beat the Americans. In the Olympic final, as they battled through an unbalanced thirteen penalties, past-game statistics clearly told them to be happy with the silver medal. But the Canadian team pushed for more and left Utah with an improved record of one for nine against the USA: they won when it truly counted. Although stats can suggest what will happen, they are only numbers representing the past. They do not have to define the future.

Dreaming big and believing in your ability to do more are essential in order to achieve new and exceptional things, but you also have to realize that you might not always achieve your goal. Not everyone can be an astronaut. Yes, hard work and passion are a big part of success, but winning the genetic lottery for physique or IQ doesn't hurt either. Yes, you can be five feet three and play in the National Basketball Association—but being six feet seven is going to make the odds a lot better for you. Sometimes the stars might really be out of your reach, but that does not mean you shouldn't see how close you can get. If you understand the reality, you will have a better sense of what you are up against.

Experience should contribute to your reality of today, but it should not limit your potential for tomorrow. In connecting your now to your future, experience and information can help you to fill the gaps by giving you an idea of the distances between the steps. As a young rower I made every crew I tried out for fairly easily—club, university, and even the junior national team; I was fit and strong. The gaps between some steps seemed small and easy, and progression came quickly. I thought my progression would always be like that, so, with only three years of rowing experience, I saw no reason not to try out for the Olympic team. Not only did I get clobbered in the attempt, I felt belittled by the coach. He said to me, "I'm glad you didn't make this team now. The Olympic team isn't the place to learn how to row; it's the place to learn how to win. Go back to your club and work on the basics, and when you are ready, we'll teach you how to win." What did he mean, "learn how to row"? I thought I knew already; after all, I'd been winning everything—until this level.

I had always been good at what I did, and then by taking a step forward, I wasn't. The women on the national team were so strong and technically proficient. I felt as if they were entrenched in their positions, and if I wanted to take the next step, I was going to have to figure out how to knock one of them out. Suddenly that next step looked bigger than any I'd ever taken. How could I possibly do *that?*

Making the team that year wasn't realistic, but what the coach said to me also made me believe that making it in the future was. He told me how to bridge the gap. Work on the basics—strength, fitness, and technique—and then I could learn how to win. How could I possibly do *that?* It is a question that should inspire us to find answers—not inhibit us from trying.

YOUR RANGE OF EXPECTATIONS

As part of the goal-setting process, it's wise to give yourself a range of expectations. It's like going to a car wash where there is a range of services to choose from—do you want the Basic, the BasicPlus, or the Super wash? As a young rower my Basic goal during selection was to make the team; I'd be okay with that. The BasicPlus goal that I would have been happy with was to be a leader in the eight. My Super goal, the great one, was to be the top starboard and in the pair with Kathleen.

You don't perform in a vacuum, and your abilities vary from day to day. The point of preparation and training is to minimize the variation, but there will always be standout great days, when giving more seems easy; average to good days; and bad days. This is also true of your competitors or teammates. Understanding that your performance can be any combination of these variations will help you perform at your optimal level for that day. Someone else may have the best result, or worst, of his or her career, and there is nothing you can do about that.

Before every race, to give us a realistic idea of what to expect, my coach, my rowing partner, and I would use the real data of our skills and speed versus those of the competition to create a race profile prediction. We did not assume that this prediction would play out exactly, but we assumed that it could. At the 1989 World Championships in Bled, Yugoslavia, I was excited about racing at the senior level for the first time. Past data would have indicated to European countries that Canadian rowers shouldn't be a threat, but we were a new team and hoped to change this perception.

Based on our racing before getting to Bled, beating East Germany and Romania was improbable. Even our greatest race wouldn't be enough to challenge them. They would have to have a really bad day for us to beat them. We could hope for that, but it was extremely unlikely.

Our data told us that we could be competitive with the West Germans, Bulgarians, and Russians. This meant that a bronze medal was possible for us. Knowing this allowed us to race smart. When the race started, we didn't panic when East Germany and Romania pulled quickly ahead. To have matched their speed and raced their type of race would have put us outside of our capabilities. It wasn't that we let them go, but we knew to keep to our race plan, which was designed to beat all the others. We knew we could do that.

We didn't win a medal, but we realized a breakthrough. We had beaten the Russians and the Bulgarians, and for the first time in many years, Canada was beating some of the "big" nations. Our fourth-place position, just 0.96 seconds off West Germany's time, proved we were becoming a legitimate threat. It was a good race and I was very proud of it, but I cannot tell you how many times I sat in my university classes the following year tapping out 0.96 on the chronograph of my Timex watch. Daydreaming and distracted from school, I went over and over everything I thought I could have done better the previous summer. Just one second faster—argh! I was left so hungry for more; I felt its power.

If we had tried to keep up with the East Germans, it's very likely that we would have ended up fifth or sixth. Keeping our expectations in a realistic range let us make the most of our capabilities.

A realistic range of expectations can be very high, if you're very confident. When I meet someone who doesn't know that I raced at the Olympics, my favourite response to the inevitable question "How did you do?" is a modest-sounding "I did as well as I could have expected." Most people then assume that I came tenth, or worse. They say that they still think it's pretty cool that at least I had the experience of going to the Olympics, and then they change the subject. On one occasion, someone followed up with me after doing some research: "You lied to me. You won at the Olympics!" With a big grin I replied, "I didn't lie. I expected to win."

SETTING A REALISTIC
STANDARD OF COMPARISON

There is a responsibility that comes with being a leader and deciding on goals for a group. In team and group situations it's not simply about each person's wants and needs. A leader needs to set goals and communicate to the group how those goals can be achieved. Getting a whole group to accept the same goal is a skill. Getting them all to want or even be passionate for it—that is an art.

To achieve group buy-in, a leader who is defining goals for a group must let the group know by what standards they will be judged. If they are being asked to believe in and strive for more, how will they know if they have achieved their goal? Not everything is measurable. How do you judge if you are a better teacher, or parent, or nurse? Is the comparison to another person, company, or country? The more clearly the image of that success is defined, the easier it is for a group to collectively see themselves creating and following a path to achieve it.

The 2010 Canadian Olympic Team had a sexy goal: be the best nation at the Winter Olympics. For the team to be successful required a collective performance from all of the athletes, in all of the events in which they were entered. To be the nation with the highest number of medals was a tough goal. It would require Canada to have a best-ever Olympic result, but the team's leaders declared it anyway. Team leaders believed that a bold goal would convey a strength, confidence, and swagger that previous Canadian teams had lacked. The leaders based their aggressive goal setting on the collective goal setting of each sports team and their own goals to create the team goal.

At the previous Winter Games, in 2006, Germany had been the top nation (defined by total medals), with 29 Olympic medals. The United States and Canada had won 25 and 24, respectively. In 2009, the pre-Olympic year, Canada topped the charts, having won 29 World Championship medals. Germany and the United States both won 28.

The 29-medal total from the 2009 World Championships was considered to be a collection of mostly good but not necessarily great results. In some events, Canadian athletes had disappointing results; expected medallists did not achieve their personally set goals. There were also unexpected medals in other events. At that time, the leaders from each sport were polled about their expectations for Vancouver in 2010. Based on those results, a total of 29 to 34 medals was probable. Considering that the high count in 2006 was 29, if Canada's athletes had another year of good results, "owning the podium" was a legitimate goal. Great results would be nice but not required.

Being the top nation was a big sexy goal that inspired all involved to try for more. In the end, the Canadian team didn't achieve its target. It is unwise to think that anything but great will do in an Olympic year. Those five rings are special, and people always rise up and do more. No one had predicted the United States would have its greatest Games ever, winning 37 medals. Germany won 30 medals, and Canada "only" 27.

All the same, Canadians could claim a different victory after Canadian athletes won an unprecedented 14 gold medals in 2010, making Canada the winningest host nation in Winter Olympic history.

Goal setting for the Canadian Olympic Team in 2008 had been a completely different story. The goal was to place in the top sixteen at the Summer Games in Beijing. This meant the Canadian team, as a collective, would need to do all this:

- Stay ahead of Bulgaria, Brazil, and Poland in the medal count.
- Do better than Cuba, Ukraine, Holland, Spain, Romania, Hungary, Greece, and Belarus. (Historically these countries have had similar results or slightly better team results than Canada.)
- Ignore the collective results of teams from Australia, Germany, Japan, France, Italy, Great Britain, and Korea. (These countries normally win 40 to 60 medals at each Olympic Games.)
- Ignore the team results of the United States, China, and Russia; they win 60 to 100 medals each, and Canada historically wins about 20.

As a team goal it was realistic but hard. It required the same type of collection of good and great results. It was hardly a sexy or inspiring goal for the leaders to pitch to the sports and athletes, let alone one for a nation to buy into. But it was the appropriate goal to set.

At the previous Summer Games, the 2004 Olympics in Athens, Canada had placed nineteenth, winning just 12 medals. For the Canadian summer team to have the same goal as its winter team—top nation—would have been reckless and extremely unrealistic.

The team's target—top sixteen—was made clear. Coaches and athletes were briefed about what to expect. They were not to compare themselves to the United States, China, and Russia, which would be winning medals and hearing their anthems played every day. Each athlete and each sport team were supported in the pursuit of their individual goals; some goals included medals, but many didn't.

After a collection of good, bad, and great days, the 2008 Beijing Olympics came to a close. Team Canada had achieved its goal: athletes had won 18 medals, and the team placed fourteenth in the medal standings. It might not have been sexy, but because it was framed as a success, fourteenth place was celebrated.

By setting clear definitions of what the team's goals were and what would be considered a success, the team was able to manage expectations, celebrate its victories, and avoid the frustration and disappointment that could have come with irresponsible predictions.

The team's future planning must eventually include competing with those nations that are winning 30, 40, 60, and even 100 medals. Observing and integrating their winning strategies could help Canada win more medals in the future. But to expect to jump from 12, 18, or 20 medals to 60 or more in a single four-year cycle is just not realistic.

DEFINING CLEAR GOALS

Clear goals should be:

- Inclusive. Participants who have had input into goal setting are more likely to buy in and understand what is wanted.

- Specific. "Win," for example, is too vague. Win what? Win how, where, and when?
- Explained. Why is winning important? Who is involved? Is there an intrinsic or extrinsic reward?
- Progressive. What other goals can be achieved en route to winning?
- Flexible. If the environment changes, be prepared to reassess, reset, and redirect.

DEVELOPING A PLAN

The first step to achieving your goal is developing a plan that outlines the path you will follow to achieve your dream. That path is your task. The second thing you need to convert those dreams into goals and achieve them is ambition. It is the magic that actually starts you moving; everything is still just an idea until you apply ambition and actually try.

Ambition drives us and unsettles us. We watch, learn, listen, and respond based on our ambition. It compels us to try harder or try more. Having dreams and creating goals for ourselves is fun, but it's not until we start applying our ambition to them that they become real and we start moving toward achievement.

Some people are very ambitious; others, not so much. That's just part of what makes us who we are. The amount of ambition applied to a goal determines how driven and hungry to improve and achieve we are—or aren't. Big goals require big doses of ambition, but ambition can also be applied to goals in small, conservative doses. Imagine that we have our own pot of ambition and that we can choose how we want to spread it around. Do we put it all toward just one or two goals? Or do we multi-task and spread it among many? Again, that is up to each individual and makes each of us who we are. When it comes to ambition, there is no right or wrong.

So why is setting a path to achieve your goals important? As Yogi Berra said, "If you don't know where you are going, you'll end up someplace else." And I'll add—or nowhere at all. It's easier to apply your ambition to the goal-setting path, which is something you can actually work on, instead of the final goal. I've seen too many people who are frustrated because they want to do or be something—but they haven't taken the time to figure out what or how.

If I had mapped out my initial plan to get to the Olympics, it might have been as straightforward as this:

1   Find sport and learn it
2   Make club team
3   Make senior national team
4   Perform better and faster than everyone else
5   Win at Worlds and Olympics

I had a path; I knew my task. The first day I took a learn-to-row class, my dream became my goal.

It amazes me to think back and realize that this was how simple I thought my path was—I was so naive! But it had to start somewhere, and sometimes starting is the hardest part. The inertia of doing nothing can be very difficult to overcome. As I progressed and learned more about what was required, I understood that I needed to add many (many!) more images to this path in order to achieve my goal—but I had started. And, as the law of inertia says, a body in motion tends to stay in motion. The more I learned, the more I learned that there was still more to learn. (And just as a body at rest tends to [contentedly] stay at rest, the less you know, the less you are aware what there is to know—which is why some auditions on TV talent shows are so hilarious! Some people really have no idea how much they don't know or how bad or off key they are!)

The number of actual steps required to achieve each of my initial steps grew exponentially as I went along my path. There were levels of club teams, levels of national teams, and levels of performance on the world and Olympic stage to master. The complexity of technique, improved fitness, advanced strategy, team selection and politics, life balance, health maintenance, and stress management was unimaginable to me as I began. Which is just as well, because had I known the size of the task, it could very well have discouraged me from ever starting.

When creating a path to achieve any goal, it is not immediately necessary to know the details of the last steps. Chances are, by the time you get close to achieving the goal, you will have had to adjust and update your path numerous times. What you do need when creating the path is to be very clear about your first step, the task that you need to work on today. As you progress, you will learn the details for the steps required in the future.

TIPS FOR CREATING A GOAL-SETTING PATH

· Have an idea of what you want to accomplish—
  the goal.
· Gather information on what steps are required.
  Talk to experienced people (at a variety of levels)
  and research the entry requirements of clubs,
  schools, associations, teams, apprentice programs,
  job applications.

- Strive to meet as many of the requirements as possible. Be most detailed about planning and executing immediate steps but have an idea of how they will connect to future steps and programs.
- Don't go blindly in. Be aware of the pros and cons of each level. Your chances of success, affordability, and return on investment must all be considered.
- Take one step at a time. Be ambitious, but don't get ahead of yourself.
- Be prepared to enjoy the path or task as much as, if not more than, achieving the final goal. It is certain that you can try; it is not certain that you will achieve a goal.

TAKING THE MOST DAUNTING STEP

Even if the goal you've chosen is simple and realistic, the first steps can be easy to put off. Often just starting is as daunting as any challenge that you will face along the way; once you start moving, you at least have some momentum in your quest for more. Those first steps along the path to what was once just a dream are both exciting and frightening. There will be an investment of your time, money, and ego. There is also the risk of failure. The phrase "biting off more than you can chew" can loom large, so it is important to remember when you are setting your goals that you need to start with only the first step—not the final one.

Goal setting is part art, part science. When it comes to chasing a dream, there is no right or wrong; there is no dream or goal too big or too small. Envisioning the path that will allow you to progress from where you are now to where you want to be requires you to combine your childlike boldness and the skills and wisdom gained from all of your experiences. Naïveté and bravery can often be mistaken for each other.

Ultimately, you will never know what you can do until you try. And although setting a goal and embarking on a plan won't always make it happen, the act of trying is what makes us grow and how we become interesting people, regardless of the outcome. Not just interesting to other people, but interesting to ourselves—which is really the important part. The power of those additional bits we try for is intoxicating; the extra effort that *more* demands of us shows us what we are truly capable of. To achieve our goals, small and large, there is work to do; we often need to be tough, dedicated, and a little lucky. But since luck occurs when preparation meets opportunity, we can control that too—if we are prepared.

3

PREPARATION

PREPARATION, training, and learning all refer to the same thing: committing time and effort to improving knowledge or abilities in order to become proficient and increasingly efficient at a given task. At least some preparation is required for everything—hobbies, business, sport, parenting, relationships. There is no task that you can't do better with a little bit more preparation. The more prepared you are, the more able you will be to take advantage of opportunities that you come across. Being prepared is the best way to be lucky.

Preparing for a goal is like filling an imaginary cup with grains of rice. Each grain of rice represents some time and effort contributed toward a goal. Your level of ambition will dictate how eager you will be to add more rice.

Grains of rice can go into the cup for physical or mental training. You need to train and prepare your mind for some tasks and your body for others. Most goals require both. Listening, co-operating, and understanding are as important as cardio, strength, and agility.

You are also doing important preparation when you would consider yourself off duty, or not working. I've been able to add grains of rice to my cup for proper nutrition, good rest and recovery, and even big laughs. These elements contributed to my ability to become the world's best rower just as rowing and lifting weights did.

As you approach your goal, your physical and mental resolve can be tested whether the goal is objective (winning against an opponent) or subjective (trying to be a good parent). If you care about your performance and are trying to do more, you will feel challenged at some point. For athletes, challenge often, but not always, comes during a specific competition or while preparing for one. For others, the challenge often comes in the form of a question. Are you prepared to answer it? Are you ready to perform? It is when you are tested that your cup and the rice in it matter. How full is the cup? How hard have you worked to get to this place? The cup of rice reminds you of your state of preparation.

Strangely, if you are lucky, you will have a goal for which the cup is impossible to fill. This happens because as you learn more, you realize that there is always more to learn. If you think there is nothing left to learn, you are probably not excited about what you are doing anymore, and it might be time to find a new goal. In an ultimate state of performance, you are keenly aware of all that you have done to prepare—the part of the cup that is full—as well as the part of the cup that you still hope to fill. This makes you confident and nervous at the same time. On the start line of every Olympic final I've been in, I knew we had done a tremendous amount of preparation, possibly more than anyone else, but I also knew that we weren't perfect. That's okay; nobody's perfect.

Because of the way I externalize almost all of my emotions, it was obvious to everyone around me that I loved to race. Because I consistently tended to race very well, many people wrongly assumed that racing was where I excelled. But I believe I excelled as much, if not more, at preparation. I knew that I could have a great race only when great preparation had come first.

One day I sat down and figured out how much time I spent preparing to race and compared it with the time I spent racing. I used low estimates for the time I spent training; when I calculated my total time spent racing, I used high estimates. For the racing figures, I even included the warm-up, which significantly increases the total time.

Training and Preparation	Racing and Competition
1.5–2.5 hrs. practice	6–8 min. per race
2–3 practices/day	30–40 min. warm-up/race
5–6 days/week	8–16 races/year
48–50 weeks/year	
720 hrs./year training (min)	12.8 hrs./year racing (max)
98% (min)	2% (max)

The result? Comparing my total training time with my total racing time in a year, I found that I spent more than 98 per cent of my time preparing to race. That meant a lot of time for putting those tiny grains of rice into my cup! Less than 2 per cent of my time was actually spent racing.

When I calculated this number for the first time, I was really surprised. Before giving it any thought, I would have expected racing to be more like 10 per cent of my time. When

I recalculated, replacing my estimates with actual to maximum estimated high training times and actual racing times, I was shocked. Only 0.01 per cent of my time as a rower was spent competing against others. More than 99 per cent was spent on preparation. There is no way that you can get good at competing if you are just killing time 99.9 per cent of the time. If you want to be a good competitor, preparation is the key. You're going to have to concentrate on filling that cup, one more grain at a time.

DON'T RELY ON NATURAL ADVANTAGES

At five feet ten, I was a bit short for a rower. Kathleen Heddle and Silken Laumann weren't tall by international standards either. At five feet eleven, these Canadian women hardly towered over the European rowers, who often stood six feet one to six feet four. In rowing, height offers an advantage because of the increased length of stroke and the leverage it provides. The rigger that holds the oar we pull works like a fulcrum, and every extra inch we can reach with the oar can result in a stroke length three or more inches longer through the water. Longer strokes mean more water pushed and, theoretically, greater boat speed.

Even though my height put me at a disadvantage, I learned to love it when I came up against tall rowers. More often than not, despite their height advantage, I could outwork them. I counted on their having a lazy work ethic because of their height. Female rowers over six feet tall had likely always been the tallest girls in their club or college programs. Good results may have come quickly to them not because they were technically accurate or pulling hard, but because of their naturally long stroke.

Sometimes the tall, "naturally talented" athletes got onto their national team with just a bit of work, relying heavily on their good DNA and their mechanical (leverage) advantage. This is where my attention to training became an edge. For me, from day one, pulling as hard as I could was all I had known. It can be easy to be good at something, but to be great requires a lot of dedicated preparation. Every day, I believed that there was something more to learn.

(Of course, not all tall girls relied only on their natural physical talents. Some of them worked just as hard as I did. If I beat them, which was really hard to do, it was simply because I was technically better!)

Every day that you work, train, or apply yourself, you earn the right to put a grain of rice into your cup. Some days will be really productive, as when you fly through your to-do list—answering all of your email, uncluttering your desk, doing the laundry, cleaning the house, getting the banking done—and these days are worth many grains. Other days seem to stretch forever, and each grain of rice that you earn seems barely noticeable. The effort for some may feel tedious and repetitious. Sometimes it may seem that you are putting the same bit of rice in the cup every day, again and again, and yet the cup does not appear to get any fuller. But the accumulation of those grains of rice, with the dedication that they represent, is just as significant as the immediately obvious things that you accomplish, if not more so.

Sometimes the cup you are trying to fill seems enormous and the grains of rice insignificantly small. For someone who has not been much of an athlete, the first week or two of training for a race may seem to result in no change. Patience and persistence are required, because it's not until somewhere in the third to fifth week that physiological changes start to show. Sometimes as you progress, you may reach a performance plateau; the body's improvements seem to stall. In these phases, you aren't even sure where to find the next grain. You want more—but where, or what, is it? Again—patience and persistence; keep plugging away, because the little bits of more will add up. Whether it's the big accomplishable tasks that line up in front of you or the small ones, as the cup fills, you will gain a sense of proficiency. Because you know you've done all that work, you will start to feel prepared.

There may be challenges, tests, and questions throughout. Sometimes it is the preparation itself that tests you. Putting some time into a task doesn't mean you are always headed in the right direction. You have to have some passion for, or commitment or connection to, your process; you have to believe in what you are doing. Just as you can put grains of rice into your cup, they can also be removed—for being careless or closed-minded, wasting time, and refusing to change.

Being resistant to the idea of change will put an end to improvement in your performance. Being open to new options and change will result in more rice in the cup. As you fill your cup, you move closer to your goal. As time passes, you gain knowledge, and knowledge is confidence. More than just understanding your task, you feel empowered to perform it. It's exciting to be good and capable and strong. As you become more capable, you also become hungry to achieve and learn more. As long as you want more, your cup is never quite full.

One of the grains of rice that I struggle with is listening. I have to constantly work to put this element back into my cup every day. If I don't think about it, I often revert back to old habits. This finally got hammered into my head when I was watching *Pulp Fiction* and Uma Thurman's character asked John Travolta what kind of conversationalist he was. Did he listen, or was he just waiting to talk? Travolta's response was that he'd like to think he was listening but he'd have to admit that he was always waiting to talk. I realized that would be my answer too, and I didn't like it. It's not the best way to learn or achieve anything. I can never take my listening grain of rice for granted.

GOOD CAN BE EASY; GREAT NEEDS TO BE EARNED

I've spoken to hundreds of groups about this cup and rice concept, and only once have I ever been asked if I really used a cup and real grains of rice. I hadn't, and I was about to tease the person who'd asked, but then I realized that the listener was looking for something more, maybe something to help with his confidence or his accountability.

Using objective measurements to chart progress and readiness is common. Heart rate monitors, training logs, and diaries are examples of excellent tools to teach self-awareness and to track performance in sport. But this question came from a high-performance athlete, someone who I assumed had already internalized this type of tracking. And yet he lacked a sense of preparedness; he had no sense of confidence.

By all accounts, this athlete had a phenomenal natural talent but also had a reputation for either putting in a spectacular performance or being a washout. The difference between his great competitions and his bad competitions was huge. It was almost as if there were no good days, just days in which he was way on or way off. He managed new challenges quickly, almost regardless of difficulty. When it was a great or maybe a good day to try something new, then the difficulty was barely a problem. When things come that easily, why would he bother to drill it?

Like the tall rowers who rely on their natural strengths, this athlete didn't always have to be tough or dedicated to get the job done. When he didn't feel "on," he would simply avoid any attempt. Natural talent can help you to be good, but only thorough and constant preparation will give you the confidence to be great—on demand. For the power of more to work, you have to want to do more on the bad days as much as you want it on the great days—even if the attempt isn't nearly as much fun on bad days and you risk failing. Being tough is a grain of rice that you earn as you train. Like all the rest of the grains, you lose it as soon as you stop being tough.

Confidence comes not from feeling able to do something only in the best of circumstances but from being reasonably sure that you can do it in any circumstance. That is why the cup is big and there are so many grains of rice. If you are going to attempt to do something really hard, you are going to need a lot of preparation and confidence. Your preparations should lead you to believe that you can be successful regardless of the situation; in sport it's referred to as "performance on demand." Regardless of fatigue, stress, poor weather, or industry upheaval, someone will always rise up and succeed on bad days.

No one had asked this athlete to push or helped him with his personal accountability when he was backing off on the not-so-great days. When he spoke to me he was struggling to be tough and was hoping that maybe a real cup and grains of rice might help. It might have been too late. By protecting and coddling his natural talent, the people surrounding this athlete had diminished his ability to be tough when it counted. Sadly, he never learned to commit himself to the grind of preparation, and a brilliant career ended before it ever really got started.

You need to be aware of your weaknesses as well as your strengths and be willing to work on them in order to progress. At the same time, it's a mistake to work only on your weaknesses. That's a quick way to suck all the fun and joy out of what you are doing. If you have a natural talent, work on it! You have a potential advantage there that few others can match. But it's a bigger mistake to ignore your weaknesses. If you find yourself repeatedly avoiding the same grain of rice, sometimes it means that this is the most important grain for you to put into your cup.

SUCCESS REQUIRES MORE THAN JUST TIME

You don't have to push hard to get high-performance athletes or elite professionals to boast about the long days they spend training. They are at the gym or office early, at it all day, and up late. They work weekends. They don't take holidays.

But there is no point putting time in if it's not going to be effective. Just running up the clock doesn't put you in a position to achieve; you don't earn grains of rice for watching a clock tick. The important thing to remember is that a bum in a seat for twelve hours a day is just a bum in a seat. More doesn't always mean more. Training and preparation have to be smart and purposeful. The quality of the time spent determines whether the grains of rice go in the cup or not. Being present and engaged in the effort is what makes the time valuable.

If you go to almost any gym across Canada, you will see people who work out regularly. You can find some people there twice a day, for hours a day. They sweat and they groan as if their life depended on it. These people might identify their families and jobs as their priorities, yet still they manage to put in gym time, lots of it. Hopefully they are as effective as they want to be, but many of these people are working out—not training. The gym is simply their passion and hobby. For some, improving their performance isn't part of their ambition. Their goal may be to look good or feel good. Perhaps it's more about the community of the gym than the fitness it provides.

A similar example is that I love to garden. Unfortunately, I have no idea what I'm doing, so everything in my garden tends to suffer, regardless of how much time I spend there. I love to garden anyway, and I spend a lot of time doing it. It's not a problem for me, because I'm just not driven for more with my garden. If I were, I'd have to put in more than just time; I'd have to put in effort, like researching and studying up on plants and soil as well.

Putting in time does not make you a martyr to your vocation or make you special. People can put in lots of time, spin their wheels, and go almost nowhere. What allows you to improve your performance and believe that you are capable of achieving great goals is the quality of your effort. For improved performance, you must demand more. You must purposefully apply yourself and make every minute count.

Using time wisely and applying effort allows you to turn big dreams into big goals. If I had to choose time or effort, I'd take less time with quality effort over more time with little effort every time. I'll earn more grains of rice and get closer to my goal that way.

THERE ARE GOING TO BE
GREAT, GOOD, AND BAD DAYS

When you set your goal, you must consider that you will have great, good, and bad days, so you must define success within a range. The same is true of your preparation; there is an ebb and flow to your ability to perform both mentally and physically.

What you have to give on your great days is of higher quality, and more efficient, than what you have to give on "just" good days. My bad days disappoint me because I always hope for more. But you need to accept that you *will* have both bad and great days. You earn grains of rice no matter what kind of day you're having. On bad days, I actually think I earn bonus grains. On those days I have to work through much more just to get the job done. When nothing comes easily, it feels as if you earn so much more. Whatever kind of day it is, you have to give 100 per cent of what you have.

You have to be aware of this ebb and flow in the people around you, too. The people you work with and for, your family, clients, observers—all will have their great, good, and bad days, and you have to trust and support that they are giving 100 per cent of whatever they have to give. On a bad day, the Olympic gold medallist kayaker Adam van Koeverden says, a single supportive comment "can turn a really crappy minus-five day into an okay plus-five day," on a scale of 10. If you berate someone who is having a bad day, even though she is giving 100 per cent of her efforts, you can destroy her confidence. This doesn't move anyone forward.

Preparation enables you to learn and improve your range of performances and to minimize the difference between your great and bad days. You have to commit all that you can to your task regardless of how you feel to earn the grains of rice for the effort. The gap between great days and bad days will be more significant for a novice than for a pro. It's why the pros can be competitive even on what they consider bad days.

IN SPORT AND LIFE, FLUKES COUNT

Australia won its first ever Winter Olympic gold medal at the 2002 Games in Salt Lake City. Steven Bradbury became an Olympic champion in the 1,000-metre short-track speed skating event. His path to the podium seemed anything but a career champion's route.

Placing third in the quarter-final should have halted his advancement in the race, because normally only the first two skaters advance. But the Canadian skater Marc Gagnon was disqualified for obstructing another racer, and Bradbury got in. In the semifinal, when Bradbury looked destined to finish fifth, with no chance to advance to the final, three skaters crashed into one another. The lucky Australian finished second and again moved on—to the Olympic final.

Realistically aware that even his greatest race wouldn't match the speed of the other four racers in the event, Bradbury just wanted to skate a great race and not be embarrassed by the margin of defeat. Still, he had the Olympic dream to be on the podium, and he had prepared to go as hard as he could. Short-track speed skaters must make many technical manoeuvres to overtake each other, and the Australian could hope that the race leaders would take some risks to win the Olympic final. Any error they made might present his only opportunity at getting onto the podium, so he'd have to be ready to take it. Although he had hoped for a miracle, no one would actually have expected the race to unfold as it did.

In the last 50 metres of the 1,000-metre race the Chinese skater made a risky move that triggered a collision, taking out *all* of the racers. All, that is, except Steven Bradbury, who wasn't near enough to the lead pack to be affected. As the last man standing, he skated through (over!) the pileup of athletes to take the gold medal. He admitted that "it didn't feel right, but I'm going to take it."

The truth about sport—and life—is that flukes do count. For all of your preparations, sometimes you really can just be in the right place at the right time. An Olympic medal can come because someone else had a really bad day. In golf it might be a hole-in-one from a ricochet off a tree; in business, a new job or a great deal can be found simply because you happened to ask the right person on the right day. It doesn't say anywhere on a business card, scorecard, or Bradbury's medal, "Got lucky."

Flukes count, but you cannot rely on them. You might be easily liked or naturally good at something, but to be respected and more than just good takes effort. Some people wait for flukes, but if you are working to achieve your ambitious goals, you need a lot more control of the outcome. "The harder I practise, the luckier I get" is the ambitious person's way of accepting flukes and luck.

CAREER CHAMPIONS
PREPARE FOR THE BAD DAYS

I have a friend who rowed for Great Britain. To say that he was a great athlete is an understatement. He won his first Olympic gold medal in 1984 and another Olympic gold at each of the next four Olympic Games. Five gold medals at five consecutive Games in a power endurance sport made Sir Steven Redgrave one of the greatest athletes in Olympic history. (It's also what made him a Sir.)

In the seventeen race seasons from 1984 through 2000, Steve was the world or Olympic champion fourteen times, missing the podium only once (1985). Steve's incredible ambition to be nothing but first was driven by his understanding of the power of more. To lead the world for well over a decade required him to constantly improve physically and technically, searching for every opportunity to do more.

I never saw or heard him boast, brag, or put others down, but when he walked into a room, confidence oozed from him; you just knew that he was a champion. After winning his historic fifth gold medal at the Sydney Olympics, instead of going out for what I'm sure could have been a hero's party, he chose to spend his time in the Olympic Village, supporting his fellow British rowers, who still had their finals the next day. It always seemed to me that Steve had a firm grasp on what was important to him.

At six feet five, weighing 230 pounds, Steve could have been an intimidating figure if he wanted to be. But unless you were in one of the boats racing him, Steve presented himself as a gentle giant, a lovely man to sit and have a chat with. On many occasions I learned something from Steve, but one incident always stands out. It's when I realized the true secret behind a career champion.

At the 1994 World Championships, Steve was racing in a pair with Matthew Pinsent. (Matthew finished his rowing career with four Olympic and ten World Championship gold medals—he is now Sir too.) After 1,000 metres they were fighting for third place. Everyone on the shoreline was commenting on how uncharacteristically bad the British pair looked.

They were racing badly, making rowing look very hard. Rowing *is* very hard, but when the best people are doing it, it should look easy. It's the same with anything. Milos Raonic serving a tennis ball at over 150 miles per hour, Usain Bolt running a 100-metre race in less than nine seconds, Donald Trump selling a building, actors, singers—whatever the task, if the performer is very good, then the performance will look easy. In this race, even though everyone knew the performers to be exceptionally good, Steve and Matt were making the race look terribly hard.

At no point in the race did it start to look easy. Steve and Matt appeared to struggle through the entire race, and yet they passed the Canadian men's pair to move into the third position. Somehow they continued to struggle right past the Italians and the Germans, who had been leading the race. It may have looked rough and ugly the whole way, but Steve and Matt were once more world champions.

In the post-race media scrum the journalists, who were used to interviewing these British athletes after a dominant win, were looking forward to questioning them from a different perspective.

The first question was about their atypical race profile. Instead of getting out to an early lead, what did it feel like to have to come from well back? Steve agreed—it had been an unusually bad race for them. He and Matt had struggled to get their rhythm and timing. There hadn't been a moment when it felt like they were together. It had felt, he said, like one of the worst rows, training or racing, that they'd had together in a long time, but they had kept at it.

The next question addressed the obvious fatigue that Matt and Steve displayed after crossing the finish line. Steve agreed again—the race had been one of the most strenuous that they'd had. He had been forced to dig down for more than he'd ever had before. Steve knew that he would be recovering from the effort for some time.

The implication of the next question rankled Steve. He was asked if they felt lucky to win the race. His answer inspires me to this day. I return to it often when I need to be reminded why preparation and training are so important. "I don't train as hard as I do so that I will just win on the good days," he said. "I train as hard as I do so that I can win on the bad days too."

This could be the mission statement for everyone who is trying to improve performance and achieve: to be prepared enough to be able to win on bad days. A career champion is the one who is ready regardless of what the external or self-inflicted conditions are, someone who always wins on a bad day. Steve doesn't disagree with the importance of luck, but he worked extremely hard to be that lucky.

EVERY DAY IS IMPORTANT

Preparation two years before the Olympics can be as important as what you do two weeks out, but it can be hard to feel the same urgency. It is easy to believe that the preparation for such a distant goal can be put off until tomorrow. And then tomorrow. Official countdowns to Olympic Games can start from thousands of days away, so what is the importance of a single day?

As part of my role as mentor to Canadian Olympic athletes, I send out mentoring messages to national team athletes who are hoping to become members of the Canadian team. My constant theme is this: take advantage of now.

In the few days and weeks before any deadline, stress levels are high and the value of a single day feels obvious. Often, just after a big event, we find ourselves wishing we'd had more time to prepare. Regardless of how far from the event date you are, treat every day as if it is important. Don't wait.

It's been said that the Summer Olympic medals are actually won in the winter and are merely picked up in the summer. Being capable of success at a Summer Olympics comes not just from racing in the summer but from the countless grains of rice earned training in the winter. The Olympic triathlon champion Simon Whitfield has referred to this work as "chopping wood and carrying water." It is the same for any task: what you will accomplish tomorrow, you must earn—through your commitment to more training and more preparation—today.

However, you must also pace yourself. At two years out, if you are "chopping wood and carrying water" with the same focus and intensity that you would apply at two months or two weeks away from a competition, you are likely to burn out. That type of energy is not sustainable; you need to work up to it. You earn grains of rice for planning thoughtfully, building from a solid foundation, and learning and practising skills, as well as for stepping up to test and challenge yourself.

If you leave your preparation to the last minute, your anxiety levels will rise dramatically. You will have a sense that you don't have nearly enough grains of rice in your cup. You risk panicking and underperforming.

Ambitious goal setting and achievement respond well to the momentum and load of more. But a single straw can break the camel's back, so patience is required as you accumulate more. As you pile on the grains of rice, you must ensure that the foundation of your preparation can sustain the load.

STRESS IS GOOD

Too often we speak of stress as if it were a great evil. The stress that comes as we push ourselves to learn and do more, the stress of competition, the stress of managing all the different tasks—we wish our lives were completely rid of it. In truth, stress is what makes us interesting people. The presence of stress indicates that we feel challenged and have a sense of commitment to our task or goal. As expressed by Alexandre Bilodeau—Olympic moguls champion and winner of Canada's first gold medal of the Vancouver 2010 Games, which was Canada's first Olympic gold on home soil—"As soon as you give meaning to what you do, there will be stress. You need to be comfortable in that stress."

We do not feel stress about things we don't care about. It may seem like a cruel joke, but the more we prepare for something, the higher our sense of consequence and our stress levels will be. But as Alex points out, it's a double-edged sword. The more prepared we are, the better we are able to manage and be comfortable with our stress. A cup that is full of grains of rice gives us confidence that we have the necessary skills to accomplish whatever it is that is causing our stress.

I have had the opportunity to speak at many schools across the country, to all grade levels. On one school visit I was speaking to about two hundred kids in grade four when I mentioned that I could get really stressed before a race. Then I stopped myself; I probably needed to explain to these ten-year-olds what stress was.

I asked them to raise their hand if they'd ever had an uncomfortable feeling, like butterflies, in their stomach before trying something new, or before a race or test in school. Without hesitation just about every child held up his or her hand. The teachers and parents, who were at the back of the room, were shocked. I was surprised too, and fascinated—but it made sense to me.

As a mentor, if I were given only one chance to communicate an idea, I would say that being stressed is normal: don't worry. Often I close my messages with "My goal will never be to add to your stress but to help you wear it well." Being stressed does not mean you won't achieve; it simply means that you care about what you do and how well you do it. What the grade fours were telling us was that fear and doubt occur naturally, at any age and at every level, not just in high-performance sport.

Stress is a result of wanting to achieve but fearing and doubting that you will. You know what you are supposed to do and want to do, and you have an idea of what you can do. Only because you care do you worry: can you actually do it?

Anxiety is a different thing. Anxiety comes only from fear of the unknown. Anxiety often has little to do with your goals. It tends to come from things you are not preparing for and haven't even begun to collect grains of rice for. If you find yourself anxious about something you have set as a goal, it's probably because you sense that there is more rice outside the cup than in. You know you are completely unprepared.

READY CAN COME AHEAD OF SCHEDULE TOO

In 1985, when I started rowing, I told a friend I would go to the Olympics in 1988. I was too naive to understand how big that goal, or the cup I'd have to fill to achieve it, really was. I wasn't afraid to dream big, and I thought I knew what I was getting into. It's no great surprise that I didn't make the Olympic team three years after learning to row.

In 1988, I matter-of-factly predicted that I would go to the 1992 Barcelona Olympics at age twenty-four. With that experience under my belt, I reasoned, I would make the 1996 team and win my first medal in Atlanta. I couldn't imagine rowing past the age of twenty-eight (that would be *so* old!), so after that I would probably retire and start a family. During the next two years of rowing, I came to appreciate that the get-to-the-Olympics cup was bigger than I had initially imagined, and the idea of winning was looking increasingly difficult—if not impossible—for North Americans. In my mind I adjusted my schedule and gave myself some more time. Not everything goes according to plan; some things go better.

In 1991, a year before the Barcelona Olympics, Kathleen Heddle and I became world champions. As the 1992 season was progressing, we established ourselves as the Olympic favourites. I was way ahead of schedule, and my goals were coming at me faster than I had expected. The plan, my collection of goal-achieving images, had me gaining Olympic experience at my first Games and *then* winning at my next Olympics. Strangely, being ahead of schedule can derail you as much as feeling that you are behind.

The ultimate answer to "Are you ready or not?" comes from the grains of rice in your cup. When we assessed our preparation, we could see we were ready. We had been able to accumulate the grains of rice we needed much faster than we had estimated. Realizing that we were ready to win took our stress levels way up, but knowing we were ready also helped me to manage them. I knew our cup was full enough to race to win, and we did.

DON'T LIMIT YOURSELF

One of my favourite stories about trusting your preparation and adjusting a plan on the fly comes from the 2006 Olympic Games in Italy. I was asked by the cross-country ski team to come to their accommodations and speak to them just before their competitions started. I was particularly excited for two of the athletes, Beckie Scott and Sara Renner. Beckie was an

Olympic gold medallist from the previous Games and a vigorous advocate for drug-free sport. Sara had been having a really strong year of racing, and I felt that her head was in a great place to have some big results in Turin.

I shared the drive to the team's residence with a young athlete I hadn't heard of before. She introduced herself as Chandra Crawford, and she told me how excited she was to be at the Olympic Games. Her dream, she said, was to finish in the top ten. Her best result, I learned, had come only recently. She'd had a top-three finish at a World Cup event, but a few of the top cross-country skiers hadn't raced there, opting to rest before the Olympics.

We spoke about how big the Olympics are: the crowds, the media, the banners and pageantry. An athlete cannot ignore how big the Games are, but I told her to realize that all that stuff is about the Olympic *Games*. She was here to race in the Olympic *competition*, and that race really is just a race.

I suggested she be like a gopher. (Jammed cats, gophers— I don't know where my mind gets this stuff sometimes!) Just as a gopher sticks its head up to make sure it's going the right way before it ducks back into its hole and digs and digs toward its goal, she should take a good look at all the Games stuff and then put her head down and focus on the competition.

About a week later, I went to watch a cross-country sprint event. It would be a quick and exciting race to watch. I arrived in time for the quarter-finals, just after the qualifying race, which isn't really a crowd pleaser. For the qualifier, each athlete races against the clock, with only the top thirty athletes (of sixty-six) advancing to the quarter-final round. For the rest of the competition, athletes would race against each other and not the clock.

Beckie had the fastest time in qualifying, so it wasn't surprising that she also won the first quarter-final. Sara finished fourth of the six skiers in her race, and sadly she would not advance. I had just turned to get a hot chocolate before the semis when I was surprised to learn there was a fifth quarter-final. I had forgotten about Chandra.

As the TV camera panned across the athletes, introducing them before their race, it was impossible to miss her. She was the only athlete on the line for this Olympic quarter-final with a massive smile. The race started and Chandra flew. As if oblivious to the magnitude of the event, she won her race by over a second and had the fastest of all quarter-final times. Chandra advanced to the semifinals, which meant she had already achieved her dream. Just standing on the semifinal start line would mean a top-ten finish. From what Chandra had told me about her goals, I could only wonder if she hadn't spent all of her energy just to get to this level.

The veteran, Beckie Scott, was still the race favourite. When the athletes were introduced for the semifinals, Chandra's smile stuck out again. Everyone else in this round, including Beckie, had a very serious and focussed—almost grim—look. Chandra looked just as focussed but she was anything but grim—she was beaming. Like a gopher fixated on the tunnel before it, Chandra looked eager to dig!

Chandra and Beckie both advanced to the finals. This meant that Chandra had now clearly surpassed her goal of top ten and would finish in the top four at the Olympics. Again, she had clocked the fastest time in the semis by a strong margin. I was concerned: if she was that far ahead of the favourites, perhaps she wasn't racing smart. Could she have anything left for the final? Did it matter, though? She had exceeded her dream.

It would have been easy for her to be completely overwhelmed and stressed by the Olympic-size pressure around her. She was so far ahead of her plans. Instead, a composed and focussed athlete with a really big smile came to the start line of the Olympic final.

Chandra controlled the race. She clearly won the gold medal. In her post-race interview she said that she had learned an important lesson from the recent World Cup race, where she had placed in the top three. Not only had she learned that she liked leading, she had discovered that she was ready to lead and to win races!

Later, when I spoke to her, I had to ask her about her smile. Where did it come from? Wasn't she nervous and scared? Of course, she said. But she explained to me that usually when she had raced before, she hadn't advanced beyond the qualifiers. Most of the time she only got to race against the clock. Chandra told me she was just so happy to be racing against *people* that she couldn't help smiling; racing was so exciting that way.

Chandra's story is a wonderful example of what happens when you refuse to limit yourself and when you recognize that you are prepared enough to adjust your goals as you go. Like a gopher, make sure you're going in the right direction, adjust as you see fit, put your head down, and go for it. It can be as simple as that.

Things change. You need to include time for assessment and reassessment in your training and racing plans. You earn grains of rice for purposeful, thoughtful actions. Sometimes you will need to raise or lower your sights. Sometimes you should expand or condense your plans. But all you can do on any given day is ensure that you are putting another grain of rice into your cup and are prepared to dig when an opportunity comes.

PERFECTION MAY BE A MYTH,
BUT IT'S WORTH TRYING FOR

To achieve more, critical analysis is essential. This is true not just in sport but in sales, artistic performances, and even our relationships. We want to know how we are doing so that we can adjust and correct as necessary. Athletes and performers can become hypercritical of their training because they are striving for the perfect performance.

If you ask athletes right after their competition how they did, they will likely be able to give you a list of things, however obvious or minute, that they would like to have done better. It's not very often that they will tell you all the things that they did right; that's just the nature of the beast.

Even Nadia Comaneci, the Romanian gymnast who earned an incredible seven perfect-10 scores at the 1976 Montreal Olympics, is quick to question whether perfection even exists. In a 2009 interview with Simon Barnes of the *Sunday Times,* she was quite clear that her beam performance, credited as being her best routine at the Olympics, was anything but perfect. "I remember that sometimes I was a bit off," she said. "I felt it during the routine. I told myself, 'No, I can't make a mistake, because this is the Olympic Games.' It was not perfect, I had done it better in training." (She had become so hypercritical of herself that she went on to say, "It was a mistake, but only I knew it. It didn't show; you can look at the routine now, you can see it doesn't show.")

Perfection may be something we strive for, but we have to accept that it's almost impossible to achieve. The type of person who has the ambition to be perfect will most likely believe that there is always a bit more to be done to achieve it. The curiosity to discover what that bit more is, and to be able to perform it on demand, comes from our ambitious drive and clear goal setting. It is what drives us toward improved performance. We are constantly satisfied and unsatisfied.

REMEMBER WHAT MATTERS

I had always imagined the Olympics would be perfect. They are the pinnacle of sport. I'd been to World Cup and World Championship regattas, but when I got to the 1992 Olympics it was different. There was more of everything, and it was bigger and brighter. Special VIP lines when we arrived at the Barcelona airport made us feel like honoured guests. The Canadian team was one of the first to arrive in the Olympic Village in Banyoles. Two hours north of Barcelona, this village was home to just the Olympic rowers and was right beside the lake we would race on. My bed was less than a hundred steps from my boat. There were banners everywhere, and theme music was playing; we were being welcomed like rock stars.

It was the Olympics, and, as I'd expected, it felt perfect —until after a few days we started to notice things. Our accommodations were pretty sparse compared with those at other regattas. We were each given five hangers, a bedside table, and a single tiny towel. Our small TV received four fuzzy Spanish channels. One of our team members was actually sleeping in an unfinished kitchen, on a cot, because there weren't enough rooms. The air conditioning in the main cafeteria tent wasn't working. Actually it was working, but they'd installed it backwards! Inside, the cafeteria was being heated. Only if you sat outside the tent could you feel a brief cold wisp of a breeze before it quickly dissipated in the stifling Mediterranean heat. Spanish heat at midday is regularly over 34 degrees, so air conditioning is essential.

I could picture previous Olympians, my sport heroes, who had worn the Canadian Olympic uniform, so when the day came that I would get my own, I was very excited. I imagined cutting-edge style and technology that would make me feel like a proud member of the greatest sporting event in the world.

It was a uniform of shock and awe. Instead of red and white we found a technicolour Mediterranean mosaic. Summer polyester blazers with massive shoulder pads (no rower needs extra shoulder padding!) were paired with matching pleated shorts and bright yellow tank tops. Huge, bright yellow clip-on "sun" earrings and white straw cowboy hats were our accessories. And, to top it all off, red pot holders in the shape of a maple leaf for us to wave around. It was hardly the height of fashion. Our self-confidence and egos would take a gigantic hit wearing these outfits.

For our casual gear, along with some oversize cotton T-shirts, we were given red Adidas Gazelles. I've been told that this same style of shoe had been given to the 1976 team. By 2000, Gazelles had become retro classics, but in 1992 they were nothing but an out-of-date shoe with no support. The only saving grace was a simple black bathing suit that had "Canada" emblazoned across the front. After every meal we would go for a swim to cool down from the sweatbox that was our dining tent.

It hardly fit the perfect Olympic image that I had been preparing so completely for; I was disappointed. The myth that the Olympics would be perfect, and that the athletes' comfort was paramount, was quashed before the start of the Games. I was still proud to be there, but my spirit sagged. It was as if I had gone behind the curtain and realized that the Wizard of Oz was really just some old man.

It didn't take long for our coach, Al Morrow, to notice that we were becoming increasingly critical of our Olympic surroundings. His response was to have us look out on the water where our competitors were training. As the Americans, Germans, and Romanians rowed by, he asked if we were ready to race them. Of course we were. Did our uniform or accommodation or anything else that we were whining about affect our ability to race them? No. Al pointed out that our task was to race at the Olympics. Our rowing was the only thing we needed to worry about; everything else was just filler. Once we remembered what was important and saw our disappointment as trivial, we got our spirits back. What we had been seeing as letdowns we started to see as humorous grains of rice that we could learn from.

The imperfection of our Opening Ceremony experience would provide me with significant lessons about the impact of small actions as well as the importance of being flexible and letting go of perfect.

Marching in at the Opening Ceremony was a distinct dream image for all of us for our Olympic journey. Like everything else, for it to become a goal we needed to create a plan. As a team we discussed the pros and cons of attending this late-night event that would be held just two nights before we started racing. None of the logistics of travel, security, meals, heat, and fatigue were conducive to great racing, but it was important to us to feel part of the Olympics and the whole Canadian team. The ceremony really was an opportunity to realize a dream. But we also had a chance to win. Seven thousand athletes could march, but how many would win? Would we risk that dream by going into Barcelona just two nights before we started to race? Some of our competitors did not go, but we did.

Even though the drive would normally take only two hours, the organizers arranged to bus all one thousand rowers from Banyoles to Barcelona starting at around 2 PM for the 8 PM event, in case of any traffic or security delays. Part of our decision making was based on the information that we would be given a meal on the bus ride in. We knew it was going to be a really long and exhausting day, but that didn't mean that we could also afford to start skipping meals.

Rowers have a reputation for huge appetites. Because we expend so much energy on the water, mealtimes are essential events. At times we consume over 5,000 calories a day. To put this in perspective, a healthy diet for a non-rowing woman consists of approximately 2,000 calories. (Male rowers can require 7,000 to 10,000 calories daily.) To eat this much food, we often have four to six meals a day.

On the day of the ceremony, we packed as much as we could into the short training day. We ate a good breakfast, got dressed in our Opening Ceremony uniform, and gathered for the bus. It was a hilarious time of taking photos and comparing uniforms with the rowers from other nations.

The buses, escorted by police vehicles and helicopters, moved slowly toward Barcelona. We took pictures of the armed guards at every bridge we went under. The Olympic security network was in full effect. We planned to eat our boxed meal just before we arrived in Barcelona, but there was a problem. There was no meal on the bus.

Our bus finally arrived at the Palau Sant Jordi stadium in Barcelona, right beside the main stadium at Montjuic, where the Opening Ceremony would take place. We couldn't speak Spanish, and the volunteers' English was poor. "Inside," they said as they pushed us into Palau Sant Jordi: "You must go inside." We assumed that they meant our food would be inside.

As part of a massive group of athletes, we were corralled inside, passing through a number of levels of security. Soon we discovered that we would not be allowed out and that there was no food available in Palau Sant Jordi. This was a real concern.

We began to question our decision making. For the last few years we had been making decisions every day that were dedicated to making this the perfect regatta experience. Now, two nights before we were racing, had we risked too much? Maintaining our blood glycogen levels was very important and surely they were going to plummet. Regret and worry began to seep into us for the first time in months as we joined over three hundred other athletes on the Canadian Olympic team who had arrived from their Olympic village just twenty minutes away.

We were trying to ignore our slight panic and increasing hunger when the Canadian team's chef de mission, Ken Read, asked how we were doing. Without question, it was exciting to be there, but we shared our concerns with him. Five minutes later we watched him pass his white cowboy hat around. He asked for contributions of spare food from all of the other Canadian athletes. At the Opening Ceremony, what athletes wear and bring is strictly controlled. We were given small fanny packs to hold a few pins, a camera, and some film; no knapsacks or large bags were allowed. It's not as if someone would have a pasta dinner or a sandwich in their pocket, so we didn't expect much. More importantly, if an athlete had packed some food, it was because he expected to need it for himself.

When Ken's hat came back, it was full. Canadian athletes had thrown in bags of nuts, apples, bananas, Mars bars, and a few packs of M&Ms. It was hardly the nutritious meal our bodies were used to, but it was enough protein and carbohydrates to keep our glycogen levels from crashing.

The significance of this simple gesture was enormous. I'm sure that not one of the athletes thought their little snack had made a big impact on the rowing team, but they had. I felt the support of the whole Canadian team and couldn't have been more confident at that moment. Our regrets were gone: we wanted the Olympic competition to begin!

Letting go of the idea that the environment around us needed to be perfect settled in with me, and some significant grains of rice filled my cup as it did. This not-perfect meal was all we needed. The energy wasted worrying about creating or maintaining the perfection of a plan is counterproductive— panicking does nothing. The pinnacle moments in our lives are no different from every other moment. Things don't always go perfectly, but they go on anyway.

SEE THE SPACES

In 1996, after winning my third Olympic gold medal at my second Olympics, I had lost the connection between chasing more and achieving my goals. I didn't feel hungry for more any longer. I was world and Olympic champion, again. What was I still chasing? Four years earlier I had asked myself the same question and the answer had been *more*. After winning my first two world and Olympic titles in 1991 and 1992, I was still absolutely hungry to learn and do more in rowing. After my third set of titles at the end of the 1996 season, I began to wonder if this was still the case. Was it me choosing to chase new goals and challenging situations, or was I letting myself be pushed by the expectations of others? Was I still in control?

If you are lucky, you get an opportunity that reminds you of your passion for your big-picture goal instead of getting caught up in the small details that we bury ourselves in. Obsessed by earning grains of rice, you lose sight of not only your cup but also the table it's on and the room that it's in.

I was a bit like that after winning the gold medal in the double sculls event in 1996. It wasn't incredible joy or physical pain that I felt upon crossing the finish line but relief: relief that we had done it, relief that I hadn't made any mistakes. The next day I won my fourth Olympic medal, a bronze in the women's quad. I watched as the crew from Ukraine celebrated their silver medal, and I was envious, not of their medal but of their joy. It made me wonder how long it had been since I had let myself experience joy like that. Had my relentless pursuit for more helped me to achieve my goal but quashed my passion for rowing in the process? I was burnt out, exhausted both physically and emotionally. I needed a change, so at the age of twenty-eight I retired from sport. Or so I thought. The next year would help to remind me of some important and really doable goals that I had once set for myself.

In my retirement I unwrapped myself from my overprotective lifestyle and learned to snowboard in Whistler, B.C. I thought this would be a good time to go and play on a mountain instead of at a lake; I affectionately referred to this season as "the year of the broken bone." Before retirement, my health had affected not only my performance but also that of my rowing partner. In this "arranged marriage," Kathleen Heddle was my dependant, and I was hers. If I got sick or injured, I took Kathleen down with me; a port is no good without a starboard. This had made me particularly sensitive to the dangers of getting injured by doing something dumb. There would be little forgiveness if I showed up with a non-rowing injury. I had pretty much turned myself into a one-trick pony in bubble wrap. This was the first thing I wanted to change. I wanted to have fun, to be carefree, and I was prepared to accept the consequences. For the first time in a long while I felt as if I could take an unplanned risk. What joy!

Living in Whistler and learning to snowboard was fantastic, but I still craved structure and focus. At the suggestion of a friend, I took a course, got certified, and—with the help of Intrawest, the company that owned Whistler Blackcomb —was quickly teaching adult beginner snowboarding. What a blast! I would free-ride in the morning with the other snowboard instructors, and then, from ten to noon each day, I'd teach a class. Saying that I snowboarded *with* the other instructors may be a bit of a stretch. The truth was that I had to do everything I could just to keep them in my sights. If this was a cup I was trying to fill, mine was still mostly empty.

Just as I hoped to progress and learn every day, I watched the other instructors improve their abilities too. They kept trying to get more height off a jump, to do a new trick, or to master a bigger feature. I watched how they would try every day but never put a timeline on their learning. They were definitely ambitious about snowboarding, but they were also patient. It made me realize that I had forgotten patience when I was rowing. I was also struck by how playful sport can be— there was so much joy.

The lifestyle I created as a snowboard instructor made a few other things apparent to me. Not the least was that I wasn't cut out to be a great snowboarder! I missed rowing— the aesthetics of it, the challenge, and the way it mentally and physically tested me. I still craved taking something that I really "got" and discovering all that was left to learn. I wanted to learn way more about rowing again.

That season, the break I took from rowing, was a gift. It became clear to me that although winning was always a very important part of my goal-setting process, the cup I was really trying to fill was to master rowing. I knew I wasn't there yet and I was still curious and hungry to know more. Winning was a result—not the goal. More importantly, I was given some further insight into my character: for me, joy and fun had been the original parts of the more that I reach for. I didn't want to let go of that goal.

I lacked the speed and agility of my snowboarding friends, so even though I was having fun, keeping up with them on fresh-snow days was next to impossible. One day, as we approached a gladed run (a run with trees on it), one of them called back to me with a tip: "Don't look at the trees." After a few small collisions with the trees—not only embarrassing but also potentially dangerous—I realized the truth of that tip. When I looked at the trees, I hit the trees. When I looked around the trees, I would make it safely past.

What I learned was this: the spaces are more important than the trees. Actively look for the spaces; don't get caught looking at the trees, because they are roadblocks and can bring our movement to a halt. Why do we so often get caught just staring at the problems around us when it is in the spaces that we find our solutions? I came to understand that this applies to more than just snowboarding; it applies to everything we do. On a gladed run, a skier or snowboarder should expect trees to be randomly present, just as we should expect challenges to occur randomly in other ventures.

From these snowboarders I took some great tools that I will use for the rest of my life. I would never have expected a group so stereotyped as anti-establishment rather than performance driven to help me in this way. Stepping away from rowing and letting myself learn from people so removed from my norm opened me to all of the different potential resources around me. Learning can come from everywhere; it is in the spaces too.

IF IT AIN'T BROKE...FIX IT ANYWAY

In 1991 the Canadian women's rowing team dominated the World Championships. The team won every event it entered, taking gold in four of six women's events. Conventional wisdom at the time considered this remarkable, since it was extremely rare for countries outside the Eastern Bloc to win in women's rowing.

You can be sure we were all geared up for a big celebration! The team gathered before the post-regatta party expecting to receive congratulations and logistics for our travels home and the packing of our equipment. But there was no champagne, no information about packing our blades or boats, and no itinerary for flights home. Instead, we were told that in three weeks, selection for next year's team, the 1992 Olympic team, would begin.

Selection? We had just dominated the rowing world. We had become the gold standard, and still we were being warned to be ready for selection? Doesn't *being* the gold standard mean that you *are* selected? Would there not be even a wee bit of grace?

In addition to the news that selection was imminent, we were told that our training methods were going to change. We had been training twice a day up to that point, but now a third session would be added so that we could include more technique, strength, and sprint work.

Change our training? We were confused. We had just demolished the competition—by dramatic margins in the pair and the four events, setting world's-best times. In the eight, six of our rowers, unlike the fully fresh crews from the other countries, had raced during the previous days. Even with that fatigue we had come from a massive deficit to win that race too. These types of victories happen only when technique is smooth and efficient. I'm usually keen on doing more, but was that much more possible?

No one had ever done what we had, and yet our coach was planning to change our training methods. I was shocked and may have been thinking, "If it ain't broke, don't fix it," when I approached our coach. Al looked me in the eye and asked, "If you aren't prepared to change, how does it get any better?" There is always a bit more, and we'd have to find it. Damn. I hate it when he's right.

If we all assume that some change is always coming, why aren't we more prepared for it? If you Google "accept change," over sixty-one million hits come up. But if you Google "antici-pate change," only two million hits come up.

Without doubt, change is going to occur. It occurs daily—in absolutely everything we do. We move along our goal-achieving path when we accept change and fill our cup with grains of rice as we do so. But if we are ready to accept change only as it happens, we will be left flat-footed and star-ing at our task as it changes and moves away from us. We then have to work extra hard to catch up. If we anticipate change *before* it happens, we can react quickly with agility; we can stay ahead of the curve.

What my coach knew was that the world was already rush-ing to match the world-leading position we had established at the Worlds in 1991. It would be unwise to get comfortable with what we had done in the past. To stay in the lead and win at the Olympics, we would have to establish the new standard for 1992. As the year drew to a close, it was impossible not to admit that Al's methods had made us more confident and faster and once again the dominant nation. I love it when he's right.

ANTICIPATE CHANGE AND CHALLENGE

Once upon a time you turned your dream into a goal by picking a route to achieve it and applying ambition. As you begin to move toward any new goal, learning and preparing yourself for each step, the path is usually clear, with a gentle, gradually increasing slope. It seems very straightforward that achieving your goal requires you to simply follow the unobstructed path ahead. As you proceed, it never seems to stay that way; things rarely go exactly as planned.

Roadblocks in the form of competitors, red tape, budget constraints, family, and corporate or social politics can sprout seemingly in the middle of nowhere and threaten your progress. In an instant, your clear and paved path can become overgrown and inhospitable. And it's the biggest roadblocks that tend to present themselves with absolutely no notice. These issues require us to change our plans, and quickly. We need to find the spaces and solutions around them.

If you accept the problem only once it reveals itself to you, you will need to check your stride and slow down. Then you can begin to consider options and change. You need to ask, "Where did *that* come from?" and "What the heck am I supposed to do now?"

Anticipating change leads to faster decision making and greater agility and flexibility at the moment you need them most. If you consider in advance potential difficulties and their solutions, you will be able to change your plan more quickly and make more efficient progress along your path. This is essential for high performance. If there is any sort of competitor involved, rapid change is essential. Instead of being surprised by an unexpected situation, your mind will simply run through its pre-established checklist: "Do I have a plan for something like this?" Check. "Can I continue?" Already done!

Challenge is no different from change. Simply accepting the challenges along your path as they appear can dramatically disturb your momentum and rhythm. Having to stop performing an action, assess, and accept each new change or challenge as it comes can be more exhausting than the action itself. Anticipating a solution is so much more powerful than waiting to accept one.

Career champions appear to be lucky at times, but it is their anticipation of change and challenge that propels them forward when everything goes crazy. Instead of slowing down, they are already attacking the task *and* revelling in a challenging environment or chaos. As you prepare for your goals, you must expect that increases in difficulty will not present themselves to you in a linear fashion. Without question, to progress or be a leader in your field, you must *anticipate* that the task will get harder. Change and challenge can come in unexpected and seemingly unmanageable clumps but so can the number of grains of rice you earn—if you're committed to the pursuit of more.

"SUCK IT UP, PRINCESS!"

It's easy to love life when everything is going smoothly. There are some people who, even though they can anticipate change and challenge, for some reason still feel compelled to complain about it. Like Eeyore, they come across as pessimistic, gloomy, and depressed. They can suck the passion and joy out of almost any task.

Once, at a 5-kilometre charity walk, I was partnered with a figure skater. As we walked together on a crisp spring day, she told me that she hated the cold. Too often, she said, the skating arena she trained in was too cold.

As an athlete from an outdoor summer sport, I found this hard to hear. Often when I had been training in Victoria, B.C., where winters are reported as "warm" for Canada, it still got damn cold! January and February can be filled with damp, bone-chilling days.

It was not unusual for us to be rowing countless kilometres in sleet, with ice forming not only on the lake's edge but also on our backs. To hear a winter athlete whose sport *requires* the presence of ice complain to me about cold arenas made my jaw drop.

"You little princess!" I thought. "It's a winter sport!" In the same way I needed to expect I would be training and competing on hot summer days, with temperatures at 35 degrees with 80 per cent humidity, she should have expected her environment to be cold.

This seemed like the opposite of tough to me. She was spoiled. Never at a loss for words for long, I simply said, "Suck it up, princess!"

I thought back to Barcelona. Going to the Opening Ceremony had been a team decision that had involved more than just when and if we would get fed. We had acknowledged that going was not the optimum way to prepare for our Olympic races, which were to start thirty-six hours after the Opening Ceremony. We had expected to be hot, tired, uncomfortable, and inadequately fed for the whole long day. The trick was to stay confident in our decision.

We chose to accept all of the challenges in order to fulfill the dream of marching with the Canadian Olympic Team. More importantly, we made an agreement to not complain about any of these choices. "Suck it up, princess" might as well have been our motto. We felt that complaining about challenges that we cannot control would do nothing but make them bigger. In hindsight, I am blown away at our wisdom, since we were all pretty much Olympic rookies.

Everything went as we'd imagined. The bus trip into Barcelona from Banyoles was long. The early dinner we'd been promised became a grab bag of snacks, far from a high-performance carbo-loading meal. We weren't given nearly enough water for the 38-degree heat.

Of course we joked about our sweat-soaked uniforms and the nutritional value of our dinner, but we never whined. People who whine always sound as if they expect people around them to fix things for them. They enable their problems to overtake them. Whiners are rarely a part of any solution. They are so very Eeyore. I don't recall hearing one complaint from my teammates.

In the end the pros—the motivation and inspiration that we gained from the Opening Ceremony—outweighed the cons of any discomfort. That team of rowers had the most successful weekend of any Canadian team in Olympic history, winning four golds and one bronze. We had been in our chosen environment; all of those "trees" had been anticipated, and we glided smoothly past.

I've talked with many teams about my idea for the motto of a career champion. I have jokingly suggested that everyone should wear a pink T-shirt under their everyday clothes, like a secret superhero uniform, with "Suck it up, princess" across the front. If you find yourself whining and bitching about things that you should have expected or that are out of your control, you might want to remind yourself of the champion's attitude.

As Brad Gushue and his curling team were about to win the gold medal at the 2006 Olympics, their team leader called my mobile. He wanted to let me know that they had been using "Suck it up" as a rallying cry to battle the flu that was running through their team. They were so ready to win that even the flu wasn't going to get in their way.

One caution about "Suck it up, princess": use it to remind yourself that you might have expected (or even chosen!) the situation you are facing. It is an internal dialogue. It doesn't work as a taunt to direct or prod others. It's not about being a bully; it's about being better yourself.

PUSH THROUGH THE ASHES

Preparation doesn't always have to be physically hard, but it certainly won't always be easy.

In 1993, after winning Olympic gold medals in the pair and the eight the year before, I returned to training for a new event, the single. No longer was I immersed in a team of women, going through the ups and downs of training as part of a group. For the first time I was going to experience all of the elements of preparation alone. At first I was pretty cocky; I had a pile of medals to prove that I enjoyed the process of preparation. I had no idea that being in a single would reveal that I had so much left to learn.

In the pursuit of more, even if we embrace and enjoy the intensity and volume of our preparations, training is sometimes designed to break us down before it builds us up.

The myth of the phoenix had been used in a fireworks display in Barcelona to represent not only the vibrancy of an Olympic Games but also the redevelopment and rebirth of this ancient European city. It was an incredible metaphor for both. About six months after I watched that incredible display of light and sound, I also saw how this myth could be applied to my confidence and preparations. I began to see that the journey for those trying to achieve a big and challenging goal is not unlike that of the phoenix. From mere ashes the bird rises to become something brilliant. It will return to ashes—only to rise to brilliance again. It is a cycle to be repeated, time and again.

I had always imagined that training through the constant wet and damp winters of Victoria allowed me to earn "martyr badges" that athletes from warmer climates would never understand. I thought that since I could suffer through those inhospitable winters I was pretty tough. Those martyr badges, like the badges I earned as a Brownie, proved (to me) that I was ready, that I was a survivor. It's one thing to push against and through external challenges; it's quite another to push through internal ones.

That March, the days were getting warm and sunny, but my boat felt sluggish and was going slowly. I had been working hard all winter, but suddenly I had really poor boat speed. I felt confused and embarrassed. It was like that for a week. I would go to training and try, but trying my hardest felt terribly slow. Finally, it was too much; in the middle of the lake, I broke into tears. How could I ever have won anything if I was this slow now? I was convinced that all of my successes had been flukes; I had never felt so useless. I had recently achieved all of my dreams; why then did I feel so terrible?

It was my teammates, from all of the other crews on the water, who helped me through my funk. In discussion we discovered that I wasn't the only one who had been through a tough time. Almost everyone has struggled in the spring. Looking through our old journals we found a common theme: we had gone through a similar low every spring.

Spring is when we experience the highest combination of volume and intensity in our preparations. This combination forms an important part of the annual training cycle and is designed to stretch us physically and mentally. The subsequent training cycle would see a decrease in volume as we tapered for racing. Through experience I recognized that spring was designed to crush me. That expectation and the knowledge that it had worked for me in the past made being crushed way easier to tolerate. Suffering through spring and coming out the other side stronger for it gave me more than just another weather martyr badge. Persevering through my internal doubts was way more complicated than just battling the elements, and for the first time I didn't have Kathleen to lean on or vent with.

This is where the myth of the phoenix comes in. I've come to see that anyone with a big goal will likely pass through what feels like the ashes of destruction. Training is designed to make you *be* better, but the volume and intensity of the preparation can feel exhausting. At some stages, studying for an exam can make you feel as if you know less instead of more. As you work on a presentation or a report, you may feel that you will never find the best way to get your message across or perhaps even discover what that message is. Exhaustion breaks you down and takes your confidence with it. It can suck your spirit dry.

Having trust in your preparation and the cycles that it moves through helps you rise up and out of the ashes you may find yourself in. Accepting and anticipating that any worthwhile achievement will involve some measure of doubt or struggle is a powerful step. It earns you important grains of rice as you proceed toward accomplishing something great.

4

TEAMWORK

O N an automobile assembly line, each person is responsible for one task, and each task contributes to the goal of creating a car. If any one task is not done on time, the group must wait. If the task is done poorly, the entire team's goal is affected—the car is a lemon.

I believe that performing a task and working toward a goal are slightly different. An individual can complete a task, but there is a team behind the achievement of a goal. To achieve more, we need help; reaching for our goals requires a collective effort.

Everyone trying to achieve a goal is part of a team; a "one-man show" is usually anything but. A salesperson who is out knocking on doors and cold-calling prospective clients may feel alone performing that task but he is not without a team and support group. Countless people are likely behind the scenes, backing up his sales with accounting, administration, marketing, and product development. The lone salesperson and the support group are the team; together they are trying to achieve a goal.

LISTENING AND TALKING

Communication is the element that binds partnerships and teams together. On the flip side, lack of communication is often what drives them apart. When communication is working, we feel increased productivity and are able to manage the natural tensions arising from stress; things seem to move along smoothly. Not surprisingly, when lines of communication break down, anxiety and frustrations rise rapidly. Communication contributes massively to both goal setting and preparation; it is impossible to fill our cup without it. Communication involves as much listening as it does talking. Having a clear vision of how to achieve something is useless if you cannot convey to those around you what you need from them and, often more importantly, why. It's ever-present and omnidirectional: communication connects leader and team, teacher and student, agent and client. It flows within teams and to and from surrounding people: competitors, allies, friends, family, and support staff.

From the outside, everyone who watched Kathleen Heddle and me saw a well-oiled machine; we worked in unison with our technique, power, and timing. Behind the scenes, staying together took a lot of work; we were anything but a natural fit. Communication was something that we could not take for granted.

From the start, our partnership seemed like an arranged marriage. I was the fastest starboard-side rower, and Kathleen was the fastest port-side rower; we had no say in the matter. It's rare that people get to select who they will work with based on personal compatibility, and for rowers it's no different. More often than not, we are grouped together not because of who we are or what we want but because of what we do in our workplace. We are directed to merge our technical strengths, disregard our personalities, and just "get the job done."

What I knew of Kathleen was that she was calm and quiet. She rarely spoke up, and although I would not describe her as shy, she was definitely reserved. I was anything but; I loved to speak my mind. I was gregarious and willing to compete at almost anything. It seemed to others as if my desire to compete oozed out of me; my passion for racing was obvious.

I was disappointed to finally work my way onto the national rowing team only to find that my new rowing partner was not at all what I expected. I had hoped to be matched with someone aggressive and competitive, just like me.

To understand how partners work together, it might help to know some of the basics of rowing. Rowers travel backwards. Facing the back of the boat, we never get to see where we are going. We don't even get to see the finish line and can only trust that we are going straight at it.

There are two styles of rowing, sculling and sweep. In a sculling boat, each rower has two oars and the event names tend to sound like multiplications: single, double, quadruple (quad). Sweep is what many people call just rowing; some also refer to it as crew. Sweep athletes use one longer oar each, and their events sound like simple addition numbers: pair, four, and eight. The number of people in each boat is easily derived from the event name, except for the eight: it actually has nine people in it. The coxswain (coxie) is responsible for steering, as well as coordinating the crew's strategy and tactics.

In a pair, as in every rowing boat—and every type of team, for that matter—there is some job specialization. The person in the bow (front) of the boat is called "bow." The person in the stern (back) of the boat is called "stroke."

Stroke must set a rhythm connecting each rowing stroke (pull of the oar) in such a way that bow, and the rest of the rowers in the case of bigger boats, can follow. All communication from stroke is non-verbal, by obvious and deliberate actions only. Since bow is looking at stroke (at stroke's back, actually), bow and the rest of the crew must mimic the rhythm and pace set by stroke.

During a 2,000-metre race, rowers rely on specific calls strategically placed throughout the race; this is known as a race plan. For a crew to attack at exactly the same moment, it is essential for someone to indicate when that moment is. (Imagine being in a three-legged race in which one person takes off before the other.) Since the voice of bow will project toward stroke, it is bow who has this speaking role. (If there is a coxie, then no one other than the coxie will speak.) Bow is responsible for articulating strategy and tactics.

It doesn't take too much guessing to figure out that quiet Kathleen Heddle was stroke and I was bow.

NOT SO CHATTY KATHY

Kathleen's calmness and quietness were not traits that I associated with aggression or competitiveness. I felt that for me to achieve my ambition to become world and Olympic champion in the pair, both people in the boat had to be aggressive and competitive in their pursuit of more. I was convinced that I was going to have to find Kathleen's competitive and aggressive side. If she didn't have one, I was ready to help her get one.

When I failed to draw out the traits I was looking for in my partner, I increased the amount of talking I did in the boat. Over and above my duties as bow, I appealed to her technical side, her ego, and even her personal character.

"Quick! Quick, Kathleen. Quick!" To me, she still seemed stoic and distant instead of eager and forceful. "Come on, Kathleen! Show me more." "Let's dominate, Kathleen! Dominate!" None of my calls seemed to trigger her. I was looking for more but still wasn't getting the response I imagined was necessary for us to become champions.

I was unsuccessful at penetrating Kathleen's even demeanour, but that didn't stop me from continuing my efforts to make Kathleen competitive and aggressive. Like anyone who is not really paying attention to the people around them, I tried more of the same but harder.

Kathleen sat just four feet in front of me. The boats are narrow and the seating area is small; there are no options to move away. I was getting the sense that if she could have distanced herself from me, she would have. The gap in our communication was increasing instead of decreasing. It was hard to know if she was even listening.

I had one last tactic to try and, even though I knew I shouldn't do it (it's not in my character to be mean), I thought perhaps it was going to be the one that worked. I was frustrated. Selfishly, I just wanted *any* reaction. I started to attack her personally. I questioned her resolve and regretted it almost instantly.

Kathleen had put up with enough. She turned to me and said, "I really hope I'm not as terrible as you're making me sound." The rebuke cut straight to my core, because we both knew that Kathleen was far from terrible. I had been nasty, and now I saw myself as she did—as a bully. She was as fed up and frustrated as I was. I still felt that I needed to find some magic button to bring us together as competitive and aggressive; I just had no idea how to do it. As bow, I felt I had failed to unify our crew. We weren't communicating at all.

That season didn't finish as well as it could have. As two talented athletes we were able to get good results in the pair but not great ones; we weren't really working together. To my disappointment, our coach did not allow us to race in the pair at the World Championships. We hadn't been able to distinguish ourselves from the other Canadian pairs, so, for the second year in row, we were placed with two other girls to race in the four.

The next year, as selection for the 1991 national team was progressing, it looked once again as if Kathleen was going to be the fastest port and I would be the fastest starboard. Our coach indicated that Kathleen and I were to be put into a pair again for the coming season. Neither one of us was excited by that idea.

I wanted to row with someone dynamic like me, and Kathleen wanted to row with someone serene like her. We both said as much to Al, but he was adamant that the fastest starboard should row with the fastest port. We were both sent out of his office with the suggestion to pay more attention to what the other was doing. I left the meeting feeling that I was stuck with more of Kathleen's tranquility; she felt stuck with more of my "nattering." Would this be another frustrating year of good racing—but nothing great?

MEASURING UP

"Those who say it can't be done are usually interrupted by others doing it," said the great African-American writer James

Baldwin. I saw for myself the difference between talking and doing in 1991, the pre-Olympic year.

There are only a few objective measures that contribute to ranking starboard- and port-side rowers. I wanted to be the type of rower whom others wanted in their boat; to fit the description and be selected, I needed to have the top erg (rowing ergometer) and seat-racing results. The erg machine would test our fitness and power; seat racing (racing in a variety of pair combinations) would test our boat-moving skills and competitiveness.

There is very little joy or fun to an erg test. It involves no real travel, no sense of racing; time and the machine are the competition. An erg test doesn't require much technique but demands self-determination and power, so it is read as a measure of aggression. I was confident that I was aggressive, and so I felt I would outshine others on this test.

I applied every ounce of my physical ability and vigorously hit each stroke. When I was done I was so spent I wanted to throw up, but I was proud. It was the best score I'd seen from a Canadian woman—that is, until I looked over at Kathleen's machine. She'd beaten my best by two seconds. I was shocked. How was it possible that this calm girl could perform so well on a test that required such a high degree of aggression? I didn't know where it came from, but after a result like that, I had to acknowledge that Kathleen was not just aggressive but *very* aggressive.

The next step of selection is seat racing. This is like a round robin tournament of 2,000-metre races (on the water), where as a starboard-side rower I would race in a pair with each port-side rower. Each round of races was against the clock, but more importantly, the race time of each pair would be compared with that of all of the other combinations of pairs. To be successful at seat racing, it is important to maximize the speed of every person you race with as a pair. As we prepared for seat racing, we would have training rows in each of the combinations. I began to keep records for all of the port rowers.

I understood that the key to being the overall winner—the champion—would be to get the best race out of each partner. Doing well with great rowers like Kathleen would be relatively easy, but not everyone in this trial was great. Some were good, and some I didn't really consider to be at national team level. The biggest difference among rowers was in their consistency of performance. The spread between great days and bad days could be minimal or massive. If someone had a bad day when she was racing with me, it could have a devastating effect on my final score; I couldn't let that happen. To win seat racing, every race would count—not just the great ones.

Whether a relationship is social, business related, or family, managing each of the different relationships around us requires a different approach. Some people are high maintenance and some are low, some people require motivation and encouragement, and some people just need space. I'd learned that some of the ports wanted calls that referred to how the boat should feel; others, how it should look; and one, how it should sound. This was the key to my competitive edge; I would communicate to each port exactly what she needed, the way she needed to hear it, in order to bring the best out of each one.

It was an exhausting week, but when it was all over I felt very proud of the work I'd done physically and strategically. As I had hoped, I won my side and was the fastest starboard. I wasn't surprised to see that Kathleen had won the port side, but what shocked me was the impressive margin that she had led by. I may have won my side, but she had dominated hers. I wondered how this even-tempered girl had done that.

To be the fastest starboard I had been so crafty, so competitive. I studied Kathleen's seat racing results and considered her erg score too. Suddenly it was obvious: this person whom I had tried so hard to *make* competitive and aggressive was already both. I externalized my desire to race, but that didn't mean I had the monopoly on those traits. Kathleen had always been forceful and energetic in her own way—not mine.

Kathleen learned something too. All of the starboards had been talking to her. Without question, she preferred the less-is-more approach, but she came to appreciate that the quality of the information and direction made a difference to the quality of the workout and race. Kathleen had to admit that in among all of my nattering there had been some very high-quality calls.

ALLOWING PEOPLE TO GIVE WHAT THEY'VE GOT

Everything changed from there. I accepted that Kathleen was extremely competitive and aggressive and that she would reveal these qualities in her own way. I got quieter in the boat and stopped nattering about motivation or personal drive. (Kathleen might argue about whether I truly *stopped* nattering. But I certainly talked *less!*) She began to share her thoughts more and gave me an idea of how she felt the boat was going. Our communication changed completely.

The big lesson was to focus on people's strengths and allow them to contribute what they can contribute. I earned countless grains of rice as I learned to embrace this idea. It is so much more than just a sport lesson. Too often we want others to communicate with us in the same way we communicate with them, and that is almost never going to happen. No one is ever going to communicate or give to me in exactly the way I communicate and give to them, and that's okay. Kathleen began to respond more but she never gave me as much information as I craved. I learned not to expect more than she could give.

Our solution didn't rely just on my getting quieter and Kathleen becoming more communicative. Relationships and partnerships are not about meeting in the middle. A partnership doesn't succeed if you give only 50 per cent of what you have and get only 50 per cent of what the other person has. Giving 100 per cent of what *you* have to give is what makes relationships and partnerships work. If you have earned it, by giving respect and effort, the people around you will give you 100 per cent of what *they* have to give.

If it helps to think of it as apples and oranges, then I had apples and Kathleen had oranges. No matter what I did or said, she wouldn't have apples to give me. In hindsight, I can see that I didn't need any more apples! Two of me in the boat would not have worked, and neither would two of her. What made us a great team was the diversity of what we had to offer.

With this change to our communication, we were able to establish ourselves as the dominant pair in Canada. At last, we were complementing each other's strengths, and we protected and celebrated each other's differences instead of trying to change them. That year we went to the World Championships as a pair, and not only did we win but we set a world's-best time that stood for the next seven years. Not bad for some apples and oranges!

Communication is not simply getting your message out. How your message is heard and accepted is as important as the message itself. Taking the time to know the people you are trying to reach can only improve your communication. If you try to understand them, you can avoid patronizing or authoritarian discussions that don't get you anywhere.

People get frustrated when they feel they aren't being heard. Sometimes in conversation I'm an idea bully. I'm just so excited to tell people what I am thinking that I have no idea what they are saying. I don't admire this trait and I don't do it on purpose, but I'm aware that I do it all too often. It's a grain of rice that I struggle with constantly; I must remind myself over and over again to listen. (Ironically, reminding myself to listen sometimes gets in the way of my listening.)

If a message is delivered poorly, teammates won't understand the expectations for going after more. People want to know what they are chasing and how they'll do it. For the essence of your message to get across and for it to contribute to performance, it must be tailored to the receiver more than to the sender.

BEHIND EVERY GREAT TEAM

In achieving a goal, teams consist of two member groups: the performer and the support group. Both groups have important and unique tasks to perform, and together they form a functioning team. The task of the performer group is to present or perform a final product, such as a race, a presentation, a lesson plan, or a play. This group may be one individual or a partnership of two or more. The support group's role is to ensure that the performer or performers are able to perform their task. Support tasks can contribute to the final product directly or indirectly. Coaches, equipment technicians, and physiotherapists are examples of this essential group in sport. Accounting, logistics, marketing, and administration provide essential support for business.

There may be ten performers and one support member, or there may be hundreds of support members for a lone performer. The performer-to-support-group ratio is not set. The construction of a team depends on the goal they share, and their ability to achieve their goal depends on effective teamwork.

Communication is essential within each group and between the two. Hand-in-glove collaboration is the key to achieving the goal efficiently and effectively. Although you may feel a heightened sense of accountability to the people that you work with directly, you need to be aware of work being done by the whole team. Everyone must have a strong understanding of how and when the performers will act together, just as everyone needs to know how and when the support group will contribute.

As I learned with Kathleen, people are different, and they work and perform differently. Associations, offices, and sport teams combine many different personalities. Some may be gregarious and obvious, like me; others may be quiet and reserved, like Kathleen. Some people are independently driven to try for more, while others are comfortable with letting inspiration and ambition come from others. If ambition or drive on a team is mismanaged, if there is too much or too little of it, the drive for more can spin out of control—or not spin at all.

A group of self-driven people working together can attain incredible momentum, but without good communication and a clear understanding of roles, it can all collapse into a catfight. An ambitious person, with a clear goal, who understands the goal-achieving path needs to know that in order to achieve, it is not always necessary to be the leader. Sometimes to achieve more, it is better to follow. How one follows can be just as important as how one leads.

SPLITTING THE TICKET

I love listening to interviews with successful people and hearing them give credit for their success to people who supported them. At the same time, I find it difficult to listen to performers who take no ownership of their performance and blame others after a poor performance.

In 2003, I found myself competing in a new sport, adventure racing. In this sport, co-ed teams of four people race four to eight days by foot, mountain bike, and canoe. There is no actual course, only checkpoints that the teams must find using a compass and a map. The race often covers 300 to 500 kilometres, and there are no scheduled stops or rest breaks. Choosing when to sleep, if you sleep at all, is part of the strategy.

I wasn't sure how I would manage being up for twenty-four hours at a time. I had never been one to pull an all-nighter when I was at university; the value of sleep always outweighed any gains from extra hours of cramming. It turned out that all I needed was a competitive goal! Twenty-four hours flew by, as did forty-eight. The exhaustion and hunger that make the difficult course so challenging are also what make the race so dramatic. Those two elements, layered with competition, can take four easygoing people and turn them into a tinderbox of duelling suggestions.

Each team has a captain. Ours, Kevin Wallace, was responsible for reading the maps and navigating the team from one checkpoint to the next. This is no easy task when you are out in a forest, with no markers or road signs. Teams are not allowed to use GPS, so even when you know you should turn east in four kilometres, you have to measure by the pace of your own steps where that four-kilometre mark is.

In 2003, we raced in the Canadian Eco Challenge in Golden, B.C. In four days my team and I covered over 350 kilometres by canoe, foot, and bike, going up and over eleven mountains. At one point, after thirty hours of continual movement, we stopped at the top of a mountain so that Kevin could go over the maps. Within seconds I was asleep; the food I had planned on eating was still in my hand, hovering by my mouth. We were so exhausted that if we weren't moving, it was that easy to fall asleep.

On a map there are many ways to get from point A to point B, and rarely is the chosen route a simple straight line. Kevin had to consider the terrain and contours on the map as he made decisions about the route our team should take. Short routes could be steeper. Other options may have less challenge but take much longer. This was a race, and as a team we had agreed that we were up for some challenge.

We worked together as much as we could. Paul would go first, breaking the trail open where needed, Kevin would follow him and guide him based on the compass and map, I kept track of our distance and pace, and Ollie, our assistant captain, would act as Kevin's sounding board. Ultimately, though, it was Kevin who made the decisions.

After almost forty-four hours of almost constant motion, Kevin brought us to a stop. The topography around us didn't match what he expected to see on the map. After a bit of discussion with Ollie, he told us that he had made a mistake. We were supposed to be in a valley that would lead us to the next checkpoint, but we were actually in the valley parallel to it. Getting out wouldn't be simple. We were going to have to backtrack over almost six hours' worth of trail.

The sun was starting to set, and we had just walked over a mountain with a dangerous summit. A glacier covered one side and it was scree, steep slope with loose rocks, on the other. None of us wanted to trek over that in the dark, so we agreed to wait another four hours until morning before we would retrace our steps to the spot where we had gone off course. Six hours in, four hours waiting, and then over six hours to return to where we would take a new direction; we had gained nothing but fatigue. We had been doing well in the race, and it was disheartening to lose so much time.

Kevin was very quiet. Adventure racing is an expensive sport, and this race had prize money for the top five teams. After the error, there was no chance that we'd recoup any of our costs. On top of the time delay, we had added a huge amount of fatigue and risked being pulled off the course if we fell too far off the pace. Our captain was inconsolable; he apologized and took responsibility for the mistake.

We were disappointed that we'd lost over sixteen hours, but we were in this together. We were a team, and we had all set out with the same idea. Accept challenge; reach for more. We all rallied around Kevin, but it was hard to convince him that we were not angry with him.

We reminded him that as we drove from Calgary to Golden, we had travelled "a bit" above the speed limit. We had agreed that if the person driving got caught speeding, we'd split the ticket. I'd like to think that if I had been driving, I'd have been clever enough to not get caught, but sometimes I do get caught. There is no reason to think that if Ollie or Paul or I had been reading the maps we wouldn't have made the same mistakes, or even more.

We finished the race almost twenty-two hours behind the leaders. I'd be lying if I said that we didn't look at the mistake compounded by fatigue and wonder, "What if?" But it wasn't a question of blame. We remained a team, and we looked forward to our next race together.

Forgive, as you would hope to be forgiven; split the ticket. It's a basic rule of a good team.

TOGETHER AS ONE

When a team is first assembled, people tend to be simply happy and proud to have made it. There is an abundance of hope in the possibilities. New faces and new ideas bring in fresh energy. After the introductions are made and we begin to settle in, we notice that all that fresh energy has also brought change to our world.

These changes may have been eagerly anticipated; something or someone new can refresh and energize a group. But in creating a new team, incorporating change can often be tricky. It may be more or less than we bargained for; people are unpredictable. A new person in a new role may mean that we have to change, maybe a lot.

For me, the formation of a new team each spring meant that I would know exactly what my specific task for the season would be. The upheaval and the stress of team selection (like a job interview) would be over. I felt relieved to know in what boat and with whom I'd be rowing, and I was able to settle into a routine. Unfortunately, it never took long for that honeymoon to be over!

Initially, we don't see the small differences in how people contribute to the work. As time passes and we become increasingly familiar with our own task and routine, our critical focus on others begins to sharpen. Hopefully we learn how to work effectively together as we realize how the performance of our teammates affects our own. But if we don't understand what each person's role is, and its value, we can become critical of what we see as the weaknesses of the people and the system around us. If we are not careful, we become less flexible, selfishly choosing to put up with less, which is the opposite of achieving more.

Every spring my coach, Al Morrow, would tell us about a couple who, when they first moved in together, were very happy—young and in love. As they settled into their new living arrangements, they perceived their little differences as quirky and cute. As they spent more time with each other and their sense of personal space decreased, tensions rose over those same quirky things. A major fight ensued for the trivial reason that one squeezed the toothpaste tube in the middle; the other, from its end. It took some work, and more communication than you would think the situation merited, but they discovered that the conflict wasn't about the toothpaste—it was about the loss of personal space. A solution was found and the toothpaste squeezing was no longer a point of friction.

To keep a team working well together, the trick is to keep the focus on the goal, not the idiosyncrasies of the process. Al wanted us to be able to normalize our relationships with each other so that we could work together and accept that people on our team would do things differently. Whether the stuff is squeezed from the middle or the end, the goal is just for it to come out of the tube.

Al's experience was that every year there would be at least one new person on his national rowing team. Any new rower, coaches, or support staff would change the balance and dynamic from the year before. Because he knew to expect a breaking-in and adjustment phase, it was easy for him to manage.

In team meetings, Al would tell us that he expected us to struggle with each other and our new team. As he said that, he also told us that he would not put up with our struggling. We did not have time to be stubborn; we had a World Championship or Olympic final at the end of every summer. We needed each other, and if we wanted to try for more each day, we would have to recognize and release the tension of the adjustment stage. Creating options to deal with change would be our way of moving through it. Only then could we perform as a team.

Rowing is a unique team sport, since there is no interaction between team members. It requires everyone to perform his or her task individually. No one can help you; there is no hand up or push forward and no encouraging look into your eyes to remind you that you can do it. It's easy to think that the way to succeed is to focus completely on yourself and let the rest of your crew take care of themselves. That could not be further from the truth.

At the same time as each rower performs the completely individual action of taking the stroke, the crew must work together in perfect unison. The timing of the blade's entering the water, the rhythm of connecting one stroke to the next, and the application of power have to be precise. When all rowers work together it's easy to work hard, but if even one person is slightly off, the task becomes much more difficult. It's like a three-legged race with up to eight people tied together. If one person falls, she will take down the whole group.

To help fundraise for the Argonaut Rowing Club in Toronto, I have coached a corporate learn-to-row program. Teams of eight signed up for an eight-week program of rowing lessons, with a regatta at the conclusion. As the crew coach, I was also the coxswain, which allowed me to be right in the boat with the inexperienced rowers.

A boat will go much faster with eight people rowing a light- to medium-powered stroke together than it would with any number of out-of-unison, very hard-powered strokes. As the coach, I needed to teach everyone his or her individual task—the mechanics of the rowing stroke. But, more importantly, to achieve our goal of winning the regatta, I needed to teach them to perform together. As they performed their own tasks, each needed to follow the person in front.

At first everyone was eager and attentive and very nervous. They listened intently; everything was new, and their learning curve was steep. I would take them through a learning progression, allowing only a few of the rowers to practise their strokes at a time, first two people together and then four. As we added more people, they would light up with excitement; the boat began to move faster. They became eager for the moment when all eight would row together. I shouldn't have laughed at them, but I often did. As a game I would silently calculate where the team's breakdown would begin; it was fairly predictable.

As the corporate group began to understand the stroke mechanics, they got less nervous and (mistakenly) more confident. That is when things would start to break down. Instead of eight people working together, they became eight people working in the same boat—which is very different. They began to focus on the power of their individual strokes and how hard they could pull, forgetting about the importance of team unison. It was like a traffic accident where one car stops quickly and all the cars behind come crashing in. At the moment they thought they would go faster, their now unsynchronized oars would get tangled and the boat would come to a stop.

I could also predict who would cause the collapse. Often it would be the person in the corporate group who had the most seniority. They were so used to giving directions and working at their own pace that they had forgotten how to fit into a group. They were so focussed on their personal performance that they lost awareness of the team; the timing of their strokes became erratic and out of sync. It became impossible for the people behind to follow. It seems the senior people weren't as familiar with listening and fitting in as they were with dictating and leading. (Ironically, it was usually those people who had brought the group to a corporate learn-to-row to foster better teamwork.) They were used to being the performers in their corporate environment, and they expected the same of themselves in the boat.

It was not always the leader who was the catalyst for these learn-to-row breakdowns. Just as often it would be the young up-and-comer, the ambitious team member who was trying to prove something to the group. This book is about encouraging people to try for more, so I can't say that trying hard is wrong. But when you try too hard, without enough knowledge of what you are doing, then things aren't likely to go as you hoped. The team would eventually progress to hard-powered strokes, but they would have to do this together.

Once they were all untangled and reset, they got back to working together. And when everyone is committed to working together, it doesn't take long for all eight oars to move as one. Then speed begins to increase, and everyone is smiling from ear to ear.

PARTNER APPRECIATION DAYS

Being good at your own task is only part of your role on the team. You need to be constantly aware of how your individual job or task fits into the group's effort to achieve its goal. Whether you are part of the performance team or the support team, to achieve the goal, you want to make things easier to accomplish, not harder.

The corporate learn-to-row provided everyone with a simple reminder: be aware of all the people around you and of how the performance of your task is affected by and affects others; they are your team. And it reminded the leaders that they needed to lead and perform in a consistent manner; the people following are counting on it.

The team that I had my first big success in was a partnership with Kathleen Heddle in the pair event. In this two-person boat, my job as bow was to articulate the strategy and tactics that we had decided on and to manage the details of the workout. As stroke, Kathleen was responsible for setting the pace and rhythm as well as steering the boat. (Her right shoe is on a pivot-and-pulley system so that if she rotates her foot left or right the boat's rudder will respond accordingly.)

As I got more comfortable and confident with my responsibilities, I began to get picky about how Kathleen was managing hers. I started to think that I could steer a straighter course or take a turn with a more efficient line than she could.

I also wanted us to take a more aggressive line heading into the dock when a workout was over. Her conservative approach ensured that the boat was safe from colliding with the dock's edge, but we would have to reach out to grab it.

Steering wasn't the only task of Kathleen's that I was critical of. I started voicing my opinions about our power application and rhythm. I wasn't convinced that her rhythm was dynamic enough. It wasn't that I thought that Kathleen was bad; I just believed that my way would be better. And I wasn't particularly quiet about my thoughts.

Eventually Kathleen and our coach had heard enough of my chirping. Al got out his tools and changed the positions of the riggers, which hold the oars, so that I could row in the stroke position. Kathleen would be in the bow. If I wanted to show Kathleen how she should be reaching for more, then this was my big chance to do it. Al didn't doubt that his original assignments were correct; he just knew that allowing us (me) to get a feel for the other's responsibilities would be an experience in partner appreciation. He said we would keep it switched for at least a week.

It's very rare for starboard rowers to get to set the pace; this was my chance to show what my idea of more was! Kathleen would have to follow me as I set the rhythm and power application. At the same time, I was a little concerned about how Kathleen would conduct the workout as bow. How could she handle my role? She was such a calm and quiet person.

We pushed off from the dock, and instantly I was having so much fun. Steering and stroking! I was confident that I would steer a perfectly straight line down the middle of the lane, and I got to put the oar into the water when I wanted to and pull hard and take it out when I wanted to. Such freedom!

After a bit of rowing, I heard Kathleen say simply, "Rhythm." I was reminded that she was behind me trying to follow my rhythm. I noticed that the onboard computer was showing that my stroke rate (number of strokes per minute) was all over the place. There was no way that Kathleen could follow my rhythm if I wasn't being consistent. I needed to be better.

I settled down and focussed on consistent rhythm. I could feel Kathleen matching me perfectly, and the boat was starting to go well. Just then there was a soft thunk. The boat had hit a small buoy that marks the lanes. I wasn't straight in the lane. Was there a crosswind suddenly? Nope, my foot was just wandering, and as a result, I wasn't steering well at all. Again, I needed to be better.

By the end of the week my hit-or-miss docking record was about fifty-fifty. When I got my aggressive approach line right, it was beautiful! We barely had to reach for the dock at all. But when I misjudged, the front of the boat would take a beating. On top of the damage to the boat, my actual rowing technique was regressing. As bow, I could manage my own technical task and my tactical one, but as stroke I couldn't multi-task as well.

Al's partner appreciation week showed me that although there were elements of Kathleen's job that I could do well, I struggled to do them all. I could handle her job, just not as well as she did. Kathleen had done a fine job as bow, but we were both very happy when Al showed up with his tools to put our riggers back where they belonged. I had a renewed respect for my partner. I was reminded that we were able to reach for amazing amounts of more when I tried to be great at my job and let her try to be great at hers. After that experiment, anytime I started to chirp about how Kathleen managed her job, Al simply brought out his tools. The threat was enough to remind me to focus on my own tasks.

YOUR TASK AS PART OF THE WHOLE

Appreciating the work and the sometimes specialized tasks that co-workers and teammates contribute to the team's goal-achieving path is as important as understanding the value of each role in achieving the goal. Whether part of the support or the performance, each person is in place for a reason, and his or her performance, although not always obvious, is in some way significant.

The first time I was invited to a sport celebrity fundraiser, I was so excited that I was going to get to hang out with sport celebs that I forgot that I was being invited as one. The first person to welcome me was the vice-chair of the Special Olympics, Jim O'Donnell, who began to introduce me around the room. Professional hockey, baseball, and football players had joined up with race-car drivers, jockeys, and Olympians to raise money at the Special Olympics Sport Celebrity Festival. I was starstruck.

Jim introduced me to Scott Goodyear, an Indy race-car driver who was a big deal that year. Scott had recently finished second at the Indy 500 by an incredibly close margin of 0.043 seconds. Jim, it turned out, was the president of Mackenzie Financial, which owned the car that Scott raced; he was, understandably, tremendously proud.

We talked about the speed of the cars and how exciting the races are. They told me about the huge team that supports the driver, and Jim made a joking comment that it wasn't a cheap sport. When I asked Jim if he had ever driven the car, he quickly said no. "I don't understand," I said. "You put all of this money into this really cool car, and you never drive it?"

"That's not my role on the team," Jim said. "I don't have to have my hands on the wheel to contribute to the race." Scott agreed. "Without Jim and the support I get, there is no car. There is no team."

They had already explained to me all the people behind the scenes that put an Indy car on the track—the engineers, mechanics, and pit crew; the team managers and sponsors. But I had still been thinking that Scott was the whole team. Neither of these guys saw it that way at all. Jim was as passionate about his role as sponsor as Scott was in his role as driver, and they absolutely understood the significance of each other's roles. They also knew that a mistimed wheel change or engine trouble as much as driver error can be the difference between success and failure. People need to understand the significance of their role, regardless of where or when it affects the path of goal achievement. I realized that this was true of all teams.

The timing of that lesson couldn't have been more important to me. After the Barcelona Olympics, Kathleen "retired" from rowing. (Thankfully, this retirement lasted only eighteen months.) For about two seconds I considered retiring, but I was still hungry to get better and learn more about rowing. Retirement wasn't really an option for me.

With Kathleen gone, I was left as a starboard without a port. There were young, talented port-side rowers coming through the system, but I knew I'd find myself unfairly comparing them with Kathleen and her amazing talent. I was going to have to do something different. It was unorthodox for a sweep rower to switch to sculling, particularly the single, but I felt up to the challenge.

In all of the crew boats, there are teammates and you are all codependent. No one rower can make an eight go particularly fast, but a slacker can dramatically slow it down. In a crew boat you cannot allow yourself to have an off day or take an easy stroke without affecting the boat's speed. It's not like a swimming team, where if you don't show up, the rest of the team can still train, or basketball, where a point guard can adapt around a player who needs to stop to tie his shoe. If you aren't giving 100 per cent, your teammates can't give 100 per cent either.

This responsibility—to perform the stroke individually while feeling intensely accountable to the group—provides motivation for rowers in crew boats to do so much more for their team than they would do for themselves. The easiest person to let down is yourself, and in the single it is obvious. I've seen rowers who can push through unbelievable physical pain when in a crew but who can't even come close when they are competing by themselves.

Racing in the single requires a special kind of rower. As a sculler, I would have one hand on the starboard oar and one on the port oar, and I'd play the roles of both stroke and bow. I would be in complete control. I would also, for the first time in my career, be the only person I was responsible for. I was afraid I wouldn't have the skills to go it alone. But what Jim and Scott had taught me about teams was that I wouldn't be completely alone; this empowered me.

I don't think I could have managed the transition into the single as well as I did without having met Scott Goodyear. Previously I had thought that a performer's role was simply to focus on the importance of his or her actions and that the role of the members of the support team was to focus on how they contribute to the performer's action. Basically, I thought being in the single would mean "It's all about me." Scott challenged that idea when he made it clear that a professional driver knows that his performance is a result of his support team. It may be only his hands on the wheel, but he knows he's not the only one driving that car to the finish line.

In crew racing, the boats are usually owned by rowing clubs, but for the single, rowers almost always own their own boats. Now that I was actually going to race the single and not just goof around in it, I needed to buy a boat. (Thanks, Dad!) My first boat's name was *Fate*. I always believed it must have been some crazy twist of fate that had led me to try rowing in the first place. It was such an unusual sport for a seventeen-year-old girl to want to take up, especially since none of my friends were interested. Then the series of opportunities that led me to the national team seemed too coincidental to be just luck. In naming my first boat I had wanted to acknowledge the randomness of how I discovered rowing, but I also figured if the name *Fate* was on my boat, then everyone else would be racing against fate. I liked that a lot.

To embrace the concept that I didn't have to work alone even as I raced alone, I named my new boat *Fate et al.* I could keep everyone on board that I needed: the voice of my coach instructing me, the strength of Kathleen, and the inspiration of my teammates were with me when I needed them, no matter how far away they actually were.

All of the people I had ever rowed with—my physiotherapist, my coach, my parents, my sponsors—had all contributed to my goal-achieving path. They were essential parts of my team, and I couldn't have achieved my success without them. Their genuine effort thrived in an environment where I gave them my true respect.

Applying your ambition to the team goal comes easily when you believe that you are valued and that those around you are giving 100 per cent. Do unto others: you get what you give. As much as some of us would like to be the driver, we don't have to have our hands on the steering wheel to play an important role in achieving great goals.

HOW MANY COOKS?

Although a working group of two is very common—we often have a best friend, a life partner, a business partner—more often we are in groups of many. There is no limit to the number of people who could be on your team, working toward a common goal. Sayings come to mind: "Many hands make light work" and "Too many cooks spoil the broth." So which is it? Can it be both? Yes, sometimes many hands make light work, but light work isn't always the most efficient or effective way to get things done; sometimes too many cooks do spoil the broth.

With a large team, the hope is that the whole will be greater than the sum of its parts. More can get done when people work together, but precision, and possibly efficiency, may go down as numbers go up. In rowing, the small boats—the singles, doubles, and pairs—have a reputation for beautiful technique and efficiency. Maintaining that exacting level of unison gets harder as the boats get bigger, but to some extent, the exponentially increased amount of power unleashed by the larger group outweighs the loss of efficiency.

To maximize your chance of success, you need to take into account the size of the group and how its members will need to work together as a team. If you are going to increase the team's size, you must ensure that your message to each person is clear.

Although I think of rowing, particularly the eights, as a team sport, I have learned from athletes in other team sports that they do not see rowing that way. Players from softball, soccer, basketball, hockey, and water polo see the teams that they are on as different from the teams I've been on. I've given this some thought, and I can see their point. The difference is that while some teams perform activities that are very straightforward, others encourage chaos.

This chaos does not arise from a lack of strategies or plans. But because each team's opponents will actively try to disrupt their forward motion with a defensive effort, they have no idea how their performance will unfold. As a team their offensive plan must respond and react to the other team's defensive interference in order to achieve any forward motion. Great offensive or defensive strategy by either team can thwart the efforts of individual players.

TEAMS THAT ARE ALL OFFENCE

Teams can be divided into two categories, chaos and non-chaos. Non-chaos teams work together to create a final result and are unhampered by their competition. For them, it's a straightforward, no-interference performance. At the completion of their task, it's as if there is a reveal, a "ta-dah!" moment. Their final result can be anything—a time of completion, a speech, or a product. Winners are determined by a comparison of their final results (which can be either objective—a time or a distance—or subjective—a personal or judging preference) with those of their opponents. Their actions are offensive, not defensive.

Rowing teams; relay teams in swimming and track; crew events in canoe, kayak, and bobsleigh; and pursuit events in cycling and speed skating are non-chaos team sports. Business is primarily a non-chaos competition. A group at a company works together to create a proposal, an idea, or a product.

Business competitors may respond, but these are almost always offensive actions. Each company's goal is for the customer to select its product as superior. When Apple and RIM released their tablet computers, the iPad and the PlayBook, each release was an offensive move. We don't imagine the late Steve Jobs or the former RIM CEO Jim Balsillie going into the other's office and smashing to bits all of the other's plans and progress. Even if one does receive a leaked or stolen concept, the response isn't to stop the other's idea but to advance their own on their terms—a decidedly offensive move.

In non-chaos environments you may be able to observe your competition, but you cannot stop them. Surge forward and counter-surge; the goal of a non-chaos team is to achieve a better "ta-dah!" moment at the end. Although the goal is often to beat other teams, it is the clock, the judges, or the volume of sales that may decide the outcome. Sometimes a group might be working together simply to create a better environment. "Ta-dah! Together we cleaned up our community." Remember, goal setting can lead to anything. There is no right or wrong.

Team members in non-chaos environments usually come to embrace repetition and routine. In the absence of a defensive assault, preparation can proceed without expectation of hindrances, and the type of performance can be anticipated. The idea of practice makes perfect and fine tuning can be applied. This is both a pro and a con. Some people will find this type of drilling monotonous; others will appreciate having the time to look for more in the details.

DEFENCE IN A CHAOS ENVIRONMENT
Teams that expect to face a defensive effort from another team rarely get to experience routine. Offensive and defensive

patterns can be practised, but come game time, the opponent will be making its best effort to not act according to expectations. In chaos environments, players and teams who can adapt and follow their intuition often outplay those who rely on theory.

A unique bond forms among team members of chaos sports. Although both chaos and non-chaos teams prepare to create something, the chaos team needs to physically repel the opposing side. Any weakness in their offensive performance will be run through by the other group's defence; united we stand, divided we fall. There is a great satisfaction to working together to repel an assault; physically breaking through and defeating an opponent can be thrilling. The artistry of strategies and the thrill of implementing them together inspire unique loyalty from players on chaos-type teams.

Chaos or non-chaos team members all have tasks to perform and roles to play. Job specialization almost always exists; it can be subtle or obvious. In the double, Kathleen Heddle and I had exactly the same task, which was to row well, but our roles as stroke and bow were different. On other teams, members may be offensive or defensive specialists, sales or marketing, golfer or caddie, but everyone is working together to do more than they did the last time.

PARTNERSHIPS

There is no maximum number of people that can be on a team, but I believe that small teams have unique and intense dynamics, particularly teams of two. Because of these dynamics, partnerships can be the best type of working group or the worst. Depending on who you are with, it can be love or hate. You don't have to like who you are working with to want to achieve the same goal. Strangely, intense antagonistic partnerships can be as effective at achieving more as the equally driven cohesive partnerships. The presence of emotional energy indicates that both partners have a passion for the task. Mediocre results are more likely to be the result of partnerships where one or both have lost (or never had) passion. Motivation and ambition are the most important ingredients in wanting to achieve more.

In 1995 the Canadian Sport Awards organization created a new category to present at its annual award dinner: "Partners of the Year." Kathleen and I were proud to win this award in 1995 and again in 1996, but at the same time we didn't understand why we couldn't compete against all of the other teams. To us, Partners of the Year seemed like the smaller, and thus easier, category to win. In hindsight, I understand why the unique working relationship between partners can be celebrated differently than the work of other teams. Partnerships involve so much more than just the tasks and roles that are performed together; communication and interdependency are profoundly intense. One person's ability to perform relies on the other person's precise execution of his or her task.

On occasion messages will be delivered poorly or the receiver won't be listening; when this becomes the rule instead of the exception, performance will break down. In addition to words and actions, eye contact, body language, tone of voice, and timing all play a part in communication, particularly with partnerships. In a partnership when communication is going well, simple words or actions can signify paragraphs of information. Talking and discussing everything can be overkill, but partners need to develop routines for sharing their thoughts on what is and isn't going according to plan. In order to be able to anticipate change and challenge, a solid partnership will have taken the time to discuss the possibilities thoroughly in advance.

For large groups, coming to such agreement on the specifics of a goal and each person's responsibilities in achieving it can be logistically difficult or even impossible. Corporate teams can stretch across whole buildings, cities, or nations. Trying to include many opinions and styles can lead to a never-ending discussion. Anyone who has ever sat in on strategic planning meetings and tried to refine a simple vision and mission statement might agree. The more people who contribute to the discussion, the less focussed the conversation will be.

In comparison, the ease with which two people can come to a consensus to share the same goal and goal-achieving path makes a partnership look simple. A well-prepared partnership develops a unique ability to remain in sync and perform together. Overcoming challenges and meeting challenging goals do not happen by accident. They take an incredible amount of trust and openness—trust that you are committed and remain committed to the same goal.

Two people working together can be highly efficient. Messages and ideas are delivered directly. A law firm with just two partners may develop a very productive way of managing its caseload. Taking advantage of each one's strengths and covering for weaknesses, the partners could easily do more business than they could if they were on their own. This efficiency also creates a dependency.

When only two people are together on a team, there is no respite from the dependence on and the responsibility to the other. If one person is having a bad day, there is a limit to what the other person can do to compensate. Even their support team can do only so much. On larger teams, having more people involved in the performance of the task means greater ability to adapt and create options.

If either partner needs to leave for an extended period of time, a replacement *must* be found. One lawyer cannot do the workload of two. (Although I've been told that articling students might argue with that!) A law firm with dozens of partners has the ability to adjust: many hands make light work.

Being part of a partnership means that there is one person that you are uniquely connected to. It's not just that you can't achieve your goal without her; she can't achieve her goal without you. Once the goal and the best way to achieve it have been agreed upon, your teammate will have your back when things get tough, and you will have hers—always. When a partnership is working, there will always be someone watching and ready to pull you up and out when you are down. Sometimes, on the strength of the partnership, we work a little harder to avoid feeling in the dumps just so that our partner won't have to pull us up.

CABLES VERSUS CHAINS

Teams are composed of a variety of—hopefully—complementary people. They come together as a team not because they are similar as much as because they have a similar goal. Gregarious people can be mixed with reserved people. *Impulsive, creative,* and *dynamic* may be descriptors of some members in your working group, just as *conservative, linear,* and *detailed* are adjectives that might apply to others. At any given time, any one of these traits, depending on the circumstances, can be seen as a strength; at other times, it can be seen as a weakness. But differences are not weaknesses in and of themselves.

Including differences of opinion, perspective, or experience can make a group stronger. Everyone has a unique combination of strengths and weaknesses. Drawing from the strengths of teammates while providing reinforcement to them in their areas of weakness binds a team together. It is the combination of all elements that makes the sum more capable than the parts.

How we come together as a team and how we support each other are essential to success. Staring at our problems only makes them seem bigger. If we isolate only the perceived weaknesses in our teammates, we will find ourselves anticipating failure; the weak link in our chain is exposed.

This would not happen if the team worked as a cable instead of a chain. In a cable no individual strand needs to be substantial or perfect. The collection of strands twisted together forms an effective team. Wrapping the strengths of some around any imperfections of others protects and reinforces the whole length of the cable.

Teams that come together like a cable will improve their performance. Their ability to reach for more will increase dramatically when team members anticipate that others will have their own strengths and weaknesses, as they do themselves. A group must learn to use its strengths as reinforcement and to build on its weaknesses instead of exposing them. That is how the team's ability to achieve increases.

When I started to row with Kathleen, I struggled to keep up to the fast and smooth action with which she moved through the "finish." The finish, or release, is the very last part of the pulling phase of a rowing stroke. This action finishes one stroke and is the transition to the next. Kathleen had a remarkable ability to be quick and fluid without ever disrupting the speed of the boat.

If Kathleen's strength was at the finish, then mine was at the "catch." The catch is the part of the rowing stroke where the blade enters the water. I had a very accurate entry and dynamic power application. My blade would enter the water quickly and be able to instantly pull on the oar.

Our coach would work with us to improve these two areas. It was inefficient for us to have such a discrepancy in our techniques. On some days we worked on the finish. I found these days very challenging, since no matter how I improved, Kathleen just continued to be that much smoother and faster around the finish than I was. The opposite was true on days where we would drill the catch. I could drop the blade in and explode faster than Kathleen every time. After having been humbled while doing finish drills, I got to own the catch drills.

In rowing, being in unison, versus simply being powerful, has an exponential effect on increasing speed. Having one person with a lightning-fast catch and the other with a superb release does not result in a net gain of one whole lightning-fast stroke. Kathleen and I needed to get our timing and power application synchronized perfectly if we wanted to perform at our best.

During a particularly tough session of trying unsuccessfully to match Kathleen, I tried something new. We weren't getting anywhere training the way we were; we'd been exposing our weaknesses. Each time we worked on the catch, Kathleen's link would break, and each time we worked on the release, it was my link that would blow. I thought we should change how we were learning. We needed to stop behaving like a chain and begin behaving like a cable.

It wasn't as if she was maliciously being better than me, or that I was bad at the finish; I just wasn't able to close the gap. I swallowed my pride and asked Kathleen to slow down enough for me to match and feel her action around the turn. Once I had that down, we could work on increasing the speed—together. Hopefully that way I would learn to match her at top speed.

It worked like a charm. We did the same thing with the catch. I slowed down the entry and power application of my blade so that Kathleen could match me. Together we ramped up the entry timing and power application until our weaknesses began to match our strengths. The increased speed of our boat as a result was incredibly exciting. When I stopped trying to cover up my weakness by proving that I could be better at something, our speed improved dramatically.

I had the good fortune of hearing the late Canadian basketball coach Jack Donohue speak. He had been the head coach of the Canadian basketball team from 1972 to 1988, and under his stewardship the team had come in fourth at two Olympics. I remember him saying to our group that his biggest peeve was when one of his players would come off the court and say something to him like, "Coach, I'm dying I'm so tired. I'm killing myself out there."

Jack scoffed. He turned to a chalkboard and drew a horizontal line, representing a level of effort, about six feet off the ground. "This is death," he said to us. "If you work up to this intensity, you will die." Jack turned back to the chalkboard and drew another horizontal line about two feet below the first. "This is sport."

Jack smiled, as we all waited for his explanation: "You aren't going to die from sport. You will pass out long before you actually die!" It was the first time anyone had said anything like that to me. What Jack taught us all is that when you think you are done, you actually have more. You almost always do.

BITCH ON BOARD

When you are pushing your teammates, respectful delivery and tone are so important. A request for more must not sound patronizing or condescending. This is difficult, because often the person asking for it is as tired as the rest of the group. In a partnership, because it is one person asking for more from another, it can easily sound like blame. In groups, it's easy to think that the request is being directed at others. *More* means *you;* there is always more to give. When you think you are doing a good job, just tell yourself to suck it up and go for great.

Being part of a team is more about working well together than it is about being friends. The important thing is that, as a group, you believe in and want the same thing.

I've seen teams made up of people who are very compatible with each other, practically best friends. This can make for a difficult working relationship, because in order to push for more, someone has to ask for it.

I watched a team of extremely strong, talented athletes train together for a year with no improvement. Every day they went out on the water for their training sessions and had good workout after good workout. They would also have good weightlifting sessions and good fitness testing. They were all very nice people and enjoyed each other's company, but they may have been too nice for their own good. Sometimes you really do need a bitch on board.

I'm not suggesting that anyone has the right to be nasty or hurl personal insults at their partners and teammates. But within each team there has to be at least one person who is willing to speak up and ask for more.

When a workout is good, someone has to step up and remind the group that good isn't great. "It was good, but our goal is to reach for great." Someone has to be ready to suggest that the team has more to give, that there is always at least a little more to give. That is the role of the bitch on board.

LEADERSHIP

The person asking for more is taking a lead, but that person doesn't necessarily have to be the only leader. Some leaders are responsible for the overall management of each team member's individual tasks and the way in which all of those individual tasks contribute to achieving the team goal.

In the preparation phase, in advance of facing an opponent or being tested, there is a risk that team members will misdirect their stress and tension inward. To avoid that, a good leader needs to keep team members connected to their personal and team tasks, roles, and goals and to remind everyone why every little bit more is important. As a team works together toward its goal, everyone must be constantly aware of what they have and haven't accomplished. Sometimes a leader will need to rein in the team because the group's desire for more is running ahead of their current training. At other times, confident that the group is ready to do more than they previously have, a leader must push them.

When and how to push a team for more requires a fine balance and understanding of the members of the team, but leadership style can vary dramatically. In the same way that I learned to focus on Kathleen's strengths and understand that she has her own role to perform, we all need to give our leaders some slack if it seems that they are not directing their attention on us all the time in the way we'd like to be receiving it.

I've been a leader within many of the teams I've been on. I've been responsible for different levels of leadership on performance teams and support teams, in sport, adventure, and business environments. But my perspective here is not that of a leader, but the viewpoint of those being led. This is what I saw and needed from the people who led me, as well as what I realized I needed to give them.

Leadership books often speak from one leader to another, and there is great value in mentor-type learning. But I believe that leaders should also take heed of what their flock has to say. How we follow depends not only on what kind of person we are but also on what kind of leader we have.

A shepherd rarely leads his flock from the front; instead he indicates the direction he wants them to take. Flocks—and teams—can be trained to be more often willing than unwilling, but as in most situations, it will be communication that makes the difference. There are leaders of every kind. Some are very outspoken, and others can be quite subtle. It's not just the strength of their message but the consistency and clarity with which it's delivered that matter. Does it make sense? Is it in line with what the group was expecting to hear? The more a leader knows her team (and the more the team knows its leader), the more likely her message will be exactly what the team needs to hear.

Every leader needs willing followers. Like good fiction, a good leader will inspire a willing suspension of disbelief from the team. If the team members are going to give 100 per cent to the leader, they must not second-guess the plan. It comes down to trust. There may be a variety of ways to achieve a goal, but a leader (with or without consultation of the whole team) must choose just one. The ability of the leader to keep her team committed to that particular goal-achieving plan, as ambitious as it may be, is what will make her a great leader.

One day after doing laundry in my house, I took my clean clothes from my basement upstairs to be folded. On my way back down I noticed I had dropped a sock. I walked right by. At various times over the next day or two I walked passed this lone sock. I noticed it, but I couldn't be bothered to stop and pick it up. I had this hope that someone else would pick it up. This would be the same someone who empties the dishwasher when the dishes are clean or takes out and then brings in the garbage cans. I always really appreciate it when someone does these things because, I have to admit, it's so much easier to be lazy and wait for someone else to do them.

Have I mentioned that I was living alone at the time?

I realized that no one was going to tell me to pick up the sock, and nobody else was going to do it. I finally said to myself that I would have to be my own somebody and pick it up myself. And then I thought about that. Had my laundry led me to realize something profound? Why was I waiting for somebody else to get the job done? I would have to be my own personal bitch on board!

Winning is like that, as are most opportunities. Somebody is going to win, so why shouldn't it be me? Why do we wait for permission or walk past opportunities that are staring us right in the face? Sometimes all that is required is for us to change our path a little, alter our overall route, and try. In order for the people leading me to be good leaders, I was going to have to let myself be led.

Leaders have to act decisively. Being your own somebody is essential for leaders. Leading requires the confidence to trust the little voice in your head—your intuition and gut instincts—and the motivation to act. Common goals will unify a group into a team; in their absence a team reverts to a group of individuals who will form their own plans. A leader must be willing to step into situations, some of which can be uncomfortable or awkward, and do—or create—something. The individual in the leader may want to hesitate and leave managing the group situation to someone else, but as the leader he pushes himself to act. The quality and consistency of those actions will be what maintains the team's suspension of disbelief, why they remain confident and committed to the plan.

All team members, to some extent, must also be their own somebody. It's not just the leader who responds proactively to situations. Everybody on a team must think and act. It might seem at cross-purposes that a flock should act independently when they have a leader to follow. But if you know your task, then you shouldn't have to be told to work on it. If you have been given a specific role, then get it done. It's not the leader's role to coddle, hold your hand, or motivate a team to want more. The leader needs to *ask* for more, but it's best if the team *wants* to give it.

To let myself be led and contribute to the team meant that, independently, I was motivated to achieve; I wanted more. I did everything I could to improve my technique, strength, and strategy. I let my coach direct me to where I should be learning. I chose to be my own somebody *and* actively follow the goal-achieving path of my team, at the direction of my leader.

FEEDBACK

Starting hard conversations is often tougher than getting through them, but when someone is doing something incorrectly, another person must speak up. A team will begin to unravel if too many things that should be said go unsaid. A leader has to be prepared to start hard conversations and address any elephants in the room, and team members have to be open to receiving some critical feedback. These conversations have to be handled in a constructive manner, but if someone isn't performing up to expectations, it is the duty of the leader to let that person know.

When leaders avoid commenting on a problem, they risk breaking that suspension of disbelief and losing the trust of the team. Inaction must not be perceived to be the result of cowardice or lack of conviction in the plan. If the group members feel that the magic of the plan is gone, then mutiny could follow.

Team members also have a responsibility to respectfully raise problems with the leader. Teams composed only of agreeable yes-men will get nowhere fast. Like everyone else on the team, the leader should strive to learn more and should be prepared for being questioned too.

Giving feedback, particularly critical feedback, can be very uncomfortable. Even when people request feedback, they don't like to hear that they aren't performing well. (Somehow "Do I look fat in this?" comes to mind. It's a genuine question, but you'd better be careful with the answer!)

Top performers will constantly seek feedback to improve but they aren't always great at receiving it. Pride in their work and a history of accomplishment tend to foster a healthy ego. Again, respect and trust are so important. The performer must feel that criticism is not intended to be personal; it has everything to do with the performance of the task. It's up to the leader to deliver it that way.

When I was an athlete, I received critical feedback daily. A rowing coach following a crew in a motorboat can observe every single stroke that we take. If we were rowing at rate of twenty-four strokes per minute, I could receive twenty-four critical comments a minute. For example, if my coach was watching my blade enter the water, I could hear, "Good, good, yes, no, late. Good. Late. Yes. No. No. No. Yes..." (Thank goodness that much feedback was not the constant norm; too much nattering just becomes noise.)

In hindsight I can see that I was being trained in more than just making a good catch; I was being trained to learn. How we receive feedback is a result of how we are taught to listen to it. The consistency of this feedback taught me that it was constructive; it was about my blade work, not about me. Learning is a skill, like any other, that we need to develop; it cannot be taken for granted. If a coach, or leader, creates a consistent method of delivering information, then the group learns how to absorb it as objective, relevant, and, above all, not personal.

As an athlete, I got so comfortable with a constant stream of critical feedback that I became uncomfortable in its absence. Having accepted the goal of being best in the world, I knew that there was always something to work on. If I wasn't told what I needed to work on next, I was failing to get closer to being the best.

As a student athlete at the University of Western Ontario, I coached the varsity women's rowing team. This is where I learned the value of giving consistent feedback.

I was coaching the varsity women's eight. Like most athletes, they were eager to learn, receptive to corrections, and keen for critical feedback. (They were just as keen for the positive feedback I gave too!) Routinely, I spread my comments out among the eight rowers, and the coxie helped me to deliver and implement the changes. A talented coxie can make the difference between a fast boat and a really fast boat, in the same way a jockey can with a horse. Coxies are responsible for strategy, tactics, and steering.

After a week or two of my corrections, the rowers' technique was coming together nicely, so I finally took the opportunity to correct the way the coxie was performing part of her task. When I gave her my feedback I was surprised by her pushback to me.

The rowers had been taking the corrections I gave them and instantly implementing them. Why, then, was my coxie, with whom I had a great working relationship, being so stubborn? Instead of doing what I asked, she spoke back and defended her way. My first reaction was anger. But instead of lashing out on the spot, I thought about it.

With the rowers, I had let them know that they were performing at a high level but that we were going to constantly refine their technique. It was important for them to know that I wasn't giving them all this critical information because they were terrible. My corrections were small changes designed to help their good stroke become great. They were conditioned to receiving my comments and appreciated them.

Had I done this with my coxie? Previously, I had given her no feedback. She had been forced to make her own decisions about what was working and what wasn't. I hadn't corrected her; I had bigger fish to fry, so I had let her good work—and it was good work—go. When I finally stepped in to push her good toward great, she wasn't expecting my critical feedback and was unprepared to receive it. Her reaction was to push back.

She told me her understanding of the plan for our workouts and how she had tried to implement it. Having heard nothing to the contrary, she thought she was doing what I wanted. She had put a huge amount of thought into it. As she defended her position, I realized that she, unlike the rowers, had taken the feedback personally. She was a talented coxie and had made sound decisions. Her way was good, but I wanted it done another way. I took the time to make clear to her why I wanted my way rather than hers. I gave her reasons that would make sense to her, and she adjusted as directed.

I realized that her defensive response had been my fault; I hadn't been a good leader to her. I hadn't taught her to anticipate and receive feedback as I had with the rowers. I had left her in a vacuum of information, and she had done the best she could with the skills and resources she had. Then I realized that I was lucky to have a coxie who challenged me the way she did. I could have been working with someone who hadn't put any thought into the way she was performing her role. It's not a bad thing to have an ambitious team member who cares enough to defend her position; she wanted more too.

Usually coxies do not receive constant critical feedback like the rest of the crew. That does not mean they don't have elements of their task to work on. I learned that I had to deliver feedback to this coxie differently from the way I gave it to the rest of the crew. I didn't become timid, but if there was a lot of time between corrections, I would have to be prepared for some discussion about why a correction was necessary.

Both of us learned something from these dialogues. We exchanged ideas based on our different perspectives of the task, and she pushed me to learn as much as I pushed her. As we progressed, she anticipated and looked forward to feedback; she still wanted to achieve more.

Later in my career, when I was training in the single, I spent a lot of time training alone. I designed my own training program and corrected and perfected my technique through drills and video analysis. I was a world and Olympic champion on the water, and at school I was about to graduate with honours in kinesiology. I felt I had the skills to know what I was doing. When I got a chance to have my coach work with me, as much as I was craving feedback, I was very quick to defend and protect the work I had done.

Brian Richardson, my coach at the time, was very good at asking how things were going and why I was doing tasks in a certain way. He encouraged me to be confident in my knowledge, even as he pointed out that I still needed to learn more. He conceded that some of my ideas were as good as or better than his. After all, I was the only one giving my problems 24-7 consideration. But he would highlight many other areas where more could be done. I really appreciated this working relationship; I felt a partner to it. I was clearly being coached but I was allowed to contribute.

There is an art to managing people. As performers become more expert, leading and teaching become collaborative. The more everyone on a team feels involved and understands why they are to perform in a certain way, the more committed they are likely to be. This has to apply to the whole team. Leaders must give some of their attention to the support group as well as the performing group. That group tends to receive little or no critical feedback; they are often left on their own to determine how to help. It's rare that a parent gets told how to cheer or a team doctor gets told where or where not to stand, but if it's important information that could affect performance, it's got to be given. If people have been doing it the wrong way for a long time, they'll probably defend themselves, but then, if their goal is the performer's best result, they will listen and make the change.

AVOIDING FEEDBACK SHOCK

In 2001, I retired from sport and found an easy pace to my days. I was on the board of a number of organizations, I spoke to corporate groups, and I had a few small jobs on TV. I was new to all of this, so after every meeting I would ask for feedback. "You did fine" was all I got. It was disappointing; I learned nothing from it. I may have gotten a standing ovation, but I wanted to know how to get better. I wouldn't have expected it but I missed receiving critical feedback.

In 2003, I took a full-time position as director of athlete programs at an entertainment attraction called Olympic Spirit. It was my first corporate job. I wasn't in a big department with a mentor or someone to follow. There wasn't much feedback or direction given. I figured things out and got a good handle on my task. After working for a few months, I was called into the executive director's office for my semi-annual performance review.

I didn't even know what to be nervous about. For six months I had done my job to the best of my abilities, and now I was going to be told if I was doing all right or not. I received some positive feedback, which I barely listened to, and then felt gutted by the bit of critical feedback that followed. It was accurate, but I took it very personally. I was a bit shocked.

I was out of practice at learning. I instantly went into a defensive mode and began to tell the executive director why I was doing things the way I had—until I realized what I was doing. I was pushing back the same way my coxie at Western had.

Many businesses are like that. Performance is reviewed and discussed only at semi-annual or annual reviews, if at all. The mandated components of the performance review, including discussion of past and future personal and corporate goals, leave little time or energy for a discussion of why and how the employee's task should get done. It becomes difficult to give and receive quality feedback if these are the only opportunities for exchange.

The more I understand what my task is and why I'm supposed to do it in a certain way, the easier it is for me to commit to trying harder; I might even be eager. Understanding that everyone's time is in demand, a leader must ensure that there are enough opportunities for casual exchanges of information. Keeping the lines open for discussion makes learning and adopting change so much easier. On the flip side, as you learn, you shouldn't always wait to be told. If you don't understand why or know how, be your own somebody and ask someone who does. Remember, this is *your* cup that you are filling with rice.

The constant feedback that an athlete can receive is similar to the feedback that comes to a sales team, which is frequent and extremely objective: a sale is made or it's not. The more frequently a sales response is provided, the less likely it is that good or bad feedback will be unexpected. Once it becomes part of our routine, it is less likely to be taken personally. This does not mean that we care any less about achieving! We may in fact desperately want to perform better and achieve more. When we can accept feedback objectively, it frees us up to address the specifics of the performance of our task. If you do look fat in that dress, it could very well be the dress's fault. All you had to do was change.

NEIGHBOUR VERSUS GURU
Does leadership style matter? Yes and no. What matters most is how leaders commit to their own style and deliver their plan to their team.

At an Olympic rowing regatta there are fourteen events: eight for the men, six for the women. Boats with one to nine people in them will race 2,000 metres, completing the course in just-over-five to just-over-seven minutes. To create even more variations, there are two weight classes for men and women: the big and powerful heavyweights and the smaller and lean lightweights. (Heavyweight is an open weight class, but the lightweight class is restricted to athletes who weigh a maximum of 158 pounds for men and 130 pounds for women.)

As the TV colour commentator for the rowing regatta of the 2004 Olympic Games, I had to explain to the viewing audience what made one crew faster than the next. What I couldn't manage to do was paint a picture of one single, perfect style, because there wasn't one. The styles used by the fourteen different winning crews were anything but similar. Power, finesse, long strokes, quick strokes, perfect unison, endurance—there were any number of factors at play. The one trait that the winning crews shared was complete commitment to their crew's particular style. A crew's style almost always comes from the coach who leads them.

I watched two great coaches imprint their incredibly different styles on their teams first-hand while training in Victoria, B.C., for the 1992 Olympics. The men's and women's rowing teams spent the winter training on the same small lake.

The men's team was coached by Mike Spracklen. Mike spoke softly, with a distinct British accent. He would pause before he spoke, and his few words were delivered like poetry, with an air of importance. People listening to him would almost lean in to get the nuance of every word.

To me, from my close, albeit outside, position, Mike seemed to present himself to his men's team as an omnipotent leader;

he was their guru. It was never questioned that he knew how to make his team champions; they had only to follow his direction *precisely.* Any deviation would result in failure.

The single driving purpose of Mike Spracklen's program was to win Olympic gold medals. I recall a story from the 1992 season when the men's team felt that the volume and intensity of the workload they carried threatened to crush them. They made a request for a break from their training, if even just for a half day. As the story was told to me, Mike considered the request and nodded. "Yes, I see," he quietly said. "Indeed you have been doing a lot of work. And I understand that you're tired and sore. You may want some time off."

They thought that this would mean they would get a break, but then Mike continued his answer. "It's *your* Olympic medal. You are free to do what *you* think is necessary. But *I* will be at the boathouse tomorrow morning. As usual." At "it's *your* Olympic medal" he had them. They wanted one so badly. They all showed up for practice the next day, and although they may have suffered, none of them *died.*

Guilt is a tremendous tool, and Mike seems to be a master at using it; he knows exactly how to tap into an athlete's own worry that he hasn't done enough. This forces an athlete to dig incredibly deep to prove, to Mike and to himself, that he has. Mike's leadership style was to demand an unquestioning commitment to the goal. His contrasting quiet and gentle delivery, which seemed incongruous next to his unrelenting message, instilled a fierce confidence and loyalty in his team.

Mike didn't give his team a great deal of information, but they knew specifically what their oars were supposed to do. If anyone ever asked the reason for a particular instruction, the answer would be, "Because it makes the boat go faster." It didn't matter if their bodies looked slightly out of unison as long as their oars moved together and went through the water faster than anyone else's. Mike alone set their path, and there was a complete buy-in to his vision. The men believed that to step away from the path set by Mike was to risk the gold medal, and they would never do that.

Al Morrow coached the women's team. I was a young athlete when I first met him. I was expecting the national team coach to have quite a bit of charisma. What I got was a normal guy, whose sunglasses and raingear weren't the coolest. He didn't care much for fashion or style, but he loved rowing—and he talked a lot. Born in Hamilton, Ontario, Al didn't have an accent to enchant his audience; he didn't come across as a guru at all.

Al's style of coaching was completely different from Mike's. He referred to himself as a "benevolent dictator." His rowers were encouraged to provide input, but whether he used it was up to his discretion. We had long daily meetings that seemed to ramble as he went through his scribbled notes. He shared a lot of information, from technical theory to boathouse maintenance. Usually he allowed the team to contribute and ask questions, making the meetings even longer.

I used to quip that our one-hour meetings had five minutes of information. It was easy to get frustrated with the meetings when all we wanted to do was get on the water. One day, over coffee, we were talking about the particularly long meeting from that morning. I listened as my teammates talked about what they had heard in that morning's meeting and realized that the important bits to them were different from the bits that I had taken in. Although it may in fact have been a one-hour meeting with five minutes of information, the method in Al's madness was that in a big group, the important five minutes would be different for each of us. What had been repetition for me had been new to others. Al gave out all the information, never assuming that any one of us knew everything.

Al focussed on every little detail of our performance, on and off the water. To Al, our body language in a meeting was as important as how we drove our legs down in the boat. These details were signs of respect to him, to the task, and, most importantly, to our teammates.

His style of coaching didn't focus so much on the goal as it did on the little details of the task. His vision was that if the group could take care of the task, and each other, then the goal would take care of itself. His athletes unanimously believed in him and his method.

When explaining a workout, Al would never say, "Today we are going to do a hard workout." It was always "Today *you* are going to do a hard workout." Al once explained that he knew he wasn't part of that effort, in the same way he wouldn't be part of any race. He knew that he was an essential part of our preparation, but we were ultimately the ones responsible for pulling on the oars. The work had to be done by us, for us, not by or for him.

Al portrayed himself as anything but an omnipotent guru. He would ask for help and learned from anything that interested him. He asked basketball, figure skating, and club rowing coaches about their performances or strategies. He never professed to know everything. On occasion with his international coaching peers, he actually played the opposite role. He presented himself as just the guy next door, acting as if he didn't really know the big answers.

This attitude proved to be an amazing resource and advantage to our team. With both the German and the American coaches, he flattered their "very strong" programs. To the German coach he commented on how efficiently they seemed to train, and to the American coach, he remarked on how strong his athletes looked. Both were guru types who underestimated Al. They responded by giving Al the specific details of their plans. We learned not only the daily mileage the German rowers were executing but also how and when their physiologists would test and monitor their lactic acid levels (which indicate muscle fatigue). The American coach showed Al his annual plan for the team's weightlifting regime, indicating the exact amount of weight being lifted by his Olympic rowers. The next year when we lined up against the German and the American teams for the Olympic final, we knew, for a fact, that we had met or exceeded their training—yet another victory for the guy next door's not-so-guru style!

That winter both teams were pushed for more than any men's or women's crew had been before. Mike's team constantly focussed on the result, Al's team on the task. This led to the inevitable discussion of who was the better coach and which program was "right." And if one was "right," did that make the other "wrong"?

The only battle that mattered to Mike Spracklen's group was winning Olympic gold. Silver would be a failure, and it would be difficult for the team to feel that there had been any value in all of the preparation they had done. I believe that this is an extremely risky style, but each one of those men believed in it to their core.

Al Morrow's vision was that the task would take care of the goal and that the little things take care of the task. It was hardly a battle cry. His attention to the tiniest detail could seem like micromanaging, and as his team we trusted his vision completely.

If Mike had convinced his team to show *him* more effort, then Al had equally convinced his athletes to show *each other* more attention to detail. The athlete profiles that CTV did for the 1992 Olympics showed the women's eight all talking about their responsibility to each other and the details, while the men's eight all talked about how Mike had convinced them that they could win. None of this is to say that the women didn't want to win a gold medal or that the men didn't want to row technically well. It's just that these elements weren't their central focus.

The tough and dedicated rowers in both programs knew that a team effort was required, but each would execute that effort differently. To watch Mike's eight race was to see a group of warriors aggressively and almost brutally pulling on their oars. In contrast, the efficiency of Al's eight showed a mastery of technique and synchronicity that could only have been achieved by relentless attention to detail. Both leaders were successful; their programs both won Olympic gold. Canada's men and women absolutely dominated the 1992 Barcelona rowing regatta.

The lesson is that there is no one right leadership style. Both coaches continue to have extremely successful careers and have repeatedly produced Olympic and world champions. Both are absolutely committed to their vision and coaching style. They both learn and develop, but what makes them great leaders is that they clearly articulate to their teams what their expectations are. Each team knows exactly what style will be expected of them.

Ultimately teamwork requires that we accept the many differences that come packaged with different people. When it comes to teams and achieving our goals, there will always be many ways to pursue more.

nd? Your high ambitions can interact with your
nd accountability, resulting in more motivation
er one or both.

WHAT DRIVES US

us hope to enjoy and care about our jobs, the
ou don't have to care to be good. I can still be
d to the details because my ambition motivates
d job—no matter what that job is. For some, it's
lity; it's simply about the reward. I've seen stu-
ve been impossible to engage in any task, who
t for quality and cared nothing for their results,
became top achievers once they identified
t motivated them to be ambitious.

ambitious to achieve our goals, the mere idea of
es us. We can be ambitious to *get* something,
prize, or we can be ambitious to *do* something,
-kilometre race or renovate a bedroom. We can
tious to *be* something, like an architect, a world
parent, or simply a good person.

has the power to magnify accountability and
, as shown in figure 3. If either of them is low,
increase either one, or both, to support bet-
nce. Ambition is the catalyst to be or do a little
s what drives the whole concept of the power of
have no ambition, you have no desire for more.
bition really just selfish? Yes, to some extent, it
actions are a result of what we choose to do. But
be a "good person" is a choice; it is a choice (and
rder one) to be honest, kind, hard-working. These
an result in our helping others more than we help

5

COMMITMENT, ACCOUNTABILITY, and AMBITION

COMMITMENT, accountability, and ambition are all connected. The first two might seem to be the same thing, but though closely linked, they are different. Commitment refers to how devoted you are to working toward your goal: Are you loyal, diligent, and dedicated to the details of the work you must do? Will you be thorough when it gets difficult? Accountability speaks to your allegiance or obligation to the task, the team, or yourself. Do you feel ownership and take responsibility for what you are doing? Ambition asks a separate question: Why are you doing this? It lets you know what is going to motivate you and why—intrinsically, because it makes you feel good, or extrinsically, because you want a more tangible reward, such as a medal, a promotion, or a contract. What is the incentive that drives you?

Understanding how these three elements interact and affect one another gives you some tools to help you accomplish your goals. Sometimes you may have to manipulate yourself to stay on track. In a performance environment, knowing how, by what, and for what you are motivated allows you to maintain your focus on the quality and quantity of work you need to do to achieve your goal.

The connection between commitment and accountability is fairly consistent, as shown in figure 1. If you feel very accountable to or responsible for the task, you usually feel very committed to all of its little details, and vice versa; one tends to encourage the other. In those situations, ambition is high. Ambition can cause high commitment and accountability or be a result of these levels. It does not always have to come first.

The opposite is usually true as well, as shown in figure 2. It's easy to be lazy (low commitment) about a task that you feel no obligation to (low accountability). This is not a great basis for performance. When commitment and accountability are low, you have little desire to be ambitious for the task and may find yourself asking, "What's the point?" Under these circumstances, you will probably not perform well or even attempt to do so.

But that's not always the case. Sometimes you may be either extremely committed or accountable to a task that isn't really yours. What would compel me to be committed to the details of a task, like a community cleanup day, that I volunteered to do? Why would I take responsibility for a job like coaching at a local rowing club that I was doing only as a

VERY COMMITTED
(extremely thorough)

LOW COMMITMENT
(lazy)

VERY COMMITTED
(extremely thorough)

LEVEL OF COMMITMENT

LOW COMMITMENT
(lazy)

LOW

FIG 1 High commitment with high ambition.

FIG 2 Low commitment with low ambition.

favour to a frie
commitment a
to improve eith

AMBITION I
While most of
truth is that y
very committe
me to do a goo
not about qua
dents who ha
made no effo
who suddenl
something tha

If we are
them motiva
like a job or
like run a 10
also be ambi
champion, a
Ambition
commitment
ambition ca
ter performa
bit more. It
more. If you
So is am
is. All of ou
remember,
often the ha
ambitions c
ourselves.

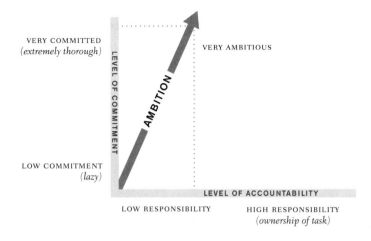

FIG 3 High ambition can increase the level of commitment even with a low level of accountability.

This is why it's so much easier to remain committed and accountable to our passion goals. These are the goals that you just know that you want; you commit to them without question. They are *yours*. Ambition for these is often high and intrinsic; being able to win the medal is way more important than possessing the medal itself. It's usually "I did it!" rather than "I've got one!"

STAYING MOTIVATED IS LIKE TRAINING A PUPPY

How you stay connected to your ambitions is not always simple; being motivated every day is a challenge. While discussing motivation with athletes preparing for the 2010 Winter Olympics, I suggested that motivation was like a puppy. Puppies can be so cute and cuddly, but when you think they're trained to come, sit, and stay, they can show you how unpredictable they really are. Training takes work, and it's about training the owner as much as training the dog. The more you and your puppy work together, the more you become in sync with each other. Even once your puppy is a well-behaved dog, it's possible that it will take off and chase a squirrel at the very moment you've said, "Stay."

Motivation works the same way. It too requires a long-term, daily commitment; you have to work at it. On the path to achieving your goals, you need to constantly tend to your motivation; it won't just stay.

When you first become ambitious for your new goal, everything is so exciting! It's a new journey, a new focus, a new passion. As you start moving toward your goal, the first few steps can be relatively easy. Starting—initiating motion—can be the hardest part; then the first few steps don't seem that bad. The slope at the base of a mountain is usually gentle and welcoming, but the higher you climb, the steeper the trail is likely to become. And so it is with paths to achieve your goals. They may be long or steep or both. To reach the top, you need to persist and keep your level of commitment and accountability to the task high. To do that, it will really help if you can maintain your motivation for your ambitions.

You might also get distracted from your goal and be redirected to another. This can be the result of losing sight of what motivated you in the first place. Sometimes you just stop caring so much. You have to accept that there are some priorities in your life that require immediate attention. Your health, family, or career may need immediate attention and take precedence over your desire to learn to paint, volunteer in the community, or run a half-marathon. You may have many goals, and you don't always get to try for the fun ones first. Sometimes a passion goal has to take the back seat to something you need more, like a job, an education, a family.

A journalist might have a dream to be a rock star. He's a talented musician, but writing the news, not playing in his band, puts dinner on the table. When he and his wife have young children, he might have to let go of some of his ambition for music as he redirects it to his writing. But putting an ambition on hold does not mean that he has to let it go completely. The level of his ambition for music will determine whether his dream to rock out will be forgotten or just set aside until he can apply his motivation to being a groovy musician again.

In the pursuit of some goals, the easy bits are sometimes harder to focus on than the challenging ones. It's easy to feel connected to pushing uphill, but even easier to get distracted when it's time to go downhill. The more accountable you are to the goal, the more attentive you will be to the "easy" phases. High accountability and commitment levels will also ensure that you remain motivated to learn even the most complex levels of the task. With the right amount of ambition, they can be seen as hurdles to be cleared on the way to your goal.

CONTROL THE VOLUME

We are in constant negotiations with ourselves. Our positive voice whispers in one ear that we can; simultaneously, our negative voice suggests all of the reasons why we can't. One of my former teammates, Brenda Taylor, says that staying motivated is really just about volume control. Exhaustion and stress work to crank up the volume of the negative voice and disconnect us from our goal. It will target any cracks in our commitment, accountability, or ambition. Our confidence has control of the positive voice, which encourages us to remain motivated. That motivation supports our ambition, which can support everything else.

The two voices are always present. To think that you can train for and perform your goals without hearing the critical chirping from your negative self is naive. But the presence of a negative voice does not mean that you are without a positive one. If you choose to hear it, it's always there.

Your negative voice feeds off all of the natural doubts and fears that you encounter. It leads you to believe that you are unworthy or incapable. The negative voice tries to magnify all of the big, scary things, making you think your grains of rice are insignificantly small in an incredibly large cup. When your confidence wanes, it is because your negative voice has temporarily blocked out your positive voice. You lose sight of what you have accomplished, and you risk being pushed off your path and becoming disconnected from what motivates you.

Our positive voice tends to stay focussed on the little things. It recognizes the value and the power of your accumulated bits of more. "Today I did this. Yesterday I did that." A collection of thises and thats is all you need to fill your cup and know that you are moving toward your goal. Your positive side remains steadfastly motivated, knowing that those little bits add up to let you believe that tomorrow you will do more.

Sometimes it takes a lot of positive voice to overpower even a little bit of negative and restore your equilibrium. Unfortunately, it is often so much easier to hear and listen to negative and critical thoughts than to the positive ones. At 6 kilometres into a 10-kilometre run, it's hard to hear the good news over all of the negative issues that your body is flagging to you. The message that you have done it before or are well trained often gets drowned out.

Just as yin exists only because of yang, the antagonistic voice may be necessary to give the positive voice strength.

But negative ideas, like insults and criticisms, often resonate and linger in our minds. We are more likely to believe someone who said that we were untalented than to believe those who said the opposite. This is why we must always do more; it ramps up the volume of the positive voice.

When you are prepared and motivated, you have little interest in acknowledging the negative voices. Your response to your doubts can serve to further encourage you. Sometimes you can surprise yourself when the response to "Do you really think you're capable of doing something that hard?" is a quick "Yes." If not yes, then perhaps, "If not today, then I'll do it tomorrow. Because I'm doing more every day."

Your drive for more may actually contribute to your negative voice. You need to be conscious of how you are feeding that beast. Always reaching for more can be twisted to diminish your sense of accomplishment—for the negative side, more is never enough. Being simultaneously satisfied and unsatisfied is the performance plan's strength and its weakness. The difference is that the positive side understands that more exists only because there is *some*.

Staying motivated involves a lot of trust—trust that you've set a path that you still believe in and want to follow. Your inner voices constantly keep checks and balances on that trust. As much as the negative voice tests you, becoming increasingly loud, trying to derail you from your path, it is your ambitious and motivated self that keeps its hands on the volume controls.

KEEP YOUR EYES ON THE PRIZE

Goal-achieving paths might as well be set on top of the board game Snakes and Ladders. Every now and then you get lucky and land on a square with a ladder that advances you farther than you expected. More often, it seems, the snake squares will show up, frustratingly sending you back to retrace the path that you've already taken. The best you can do is learn from the experience and try to control where you will land in the future. As long as you can keep your eyes on the prize, you can turn up your positive voice, which keeps you believing that the goal you have set is something you can do. Even if it's just inch by inch, your positive voice will remind you that you are moving forward toward your goal.

Although ambition can drive up your commitment and your accountability, a performance advantage definitely exists when each element is strong by itself. Ambition is like a multiplier in math; it goes nowhere with zero. You need to have some commitment or some accountability for your ambition and motivation to work. Not all goals will be driven from deep passion, and for them daily motivation will wax and wane. For great performance, I had to know what and whom I was accountable to and how I would commit to my task. Knowing why was a definite bonus.

People often asked me, "How do you stay motivated day in and day out?" I thought it was pretty obvious. My ambition was clear: I wanted to be the best rower in the world—I wanted to win at the Olympics. I think people were really looking for something that they could apply to their own daily routine. They were curious not about my motivation but about how I stayed accountable and committed to my goals day after day.

APPRECIATE THE GRIND

Contrary to popular belief, elite athletes are not necessarily happy with their careers every day. Those few athletes who make it to the elite levels of sport and find some marketing and sponsorship support have some amazing and unique opportunities, but it's still a job. For many, sport is a lifestyle choice. It is often an unpaid, under-supported, highly stressful, attempt-to-be-perfect choice. There is no job security, we are always being critiqued, and it's a constantly competitive environment.

When I was training to compete at the World Championships or the Olympic Games, it was a year-round, full-time job. "If you want to be a good runner, you run, and if you want to be a good rower, you row" was a mantra of one of our coaches; so row we did. We had three training sessions five days a week and just two on Wednesdays and Saturdays. Of course the training sessions on those two days were longer and more intense, but at least we had the afternoon off to get caught up on some sleep and laundry—how glamorous.

The national team's training centre for the women was based in London, Ontario. The city of London and the University of Western Ontario were always very supportive. It was an easy place for us to live, and more importantly, for most of the year there is a good-size lake to row on. In the winter, training on the water is impossible since, by late December, Fanshawe Lake tends to freeze up until mid-March. So we would relocate to the other national training centre and the unfrozen waters of Elk Lake in Victoria. Winter on the west coast can seem pretty balmy compared with southern Ontario. Temperatures below zero are pretty rare in Victoria, but that's not to say it doesn't get cold. The lake might not freeze often, but it frequently gets close to freezing.

I remember many January and February days when my personal mantra, with every stroke that I took, was "It's a summer sport, it's a summer sport, it's a summer sport." The dark, rainy, and chilly days that we were training in did not match the warm weather of summer regattas. I was being subjected to rain, sleet, and hail three times a day. This was my grind; it was miserable. Mentally and physically, I felt as if I was being broken down, day by day.

Our coaches designed the winter training program to be physically exhausting. To improve areas of weakness from the previous competition season, we received constant critical feedback. It was hard to stay positive when we were so tired. Worn out, beaten down, cold, and wet—I didn't like rowing on those days, and on a few occasions each winter I was pretty sure I hated it. I've talked with enough athletes from a variety of sports to know that it's impossible to feel great about what you're doing 365 days a year. There is definitely a cycle to it. For me, the way to persevere through my grind was to have a system of accountability to my teammates and to myself.

How did I manage to not give up on those hard days? What was my elite athlete trick to stay accountable and committed to my goal? I had a few methods, but I'm quick to admit that on some days what kept me going was simply that I didn't want people to think that I was a quitter.

Motivation can be drawn from everywhere. That is possibly the biggest secret that career champions have. Some days I simply loved my sport, and it was the passion for it that kept me accountable and committed to the details of technique. Some days I'd go to training because I loved the aesthetics of it—the fog rising off the water, the eagles flying overhead, our boats cutting through the water. On many days, working with my teammates to accomplish something physically hard was an opportunity I felt blessed to have. My motivation to work hard and push myself mentally and physically came easily on those days. But it is naive to expect motivation to always come from the same positive place.

Some days I was eager to be in front, and other days I just didn't want to be last, dragging down the group. There were days when I wanted to win or to be the best, but there were also days when I just didn't want to get passed or beaten. These two attitudes might seem similar, but the sources of my motivation were quite different. With one, my ambition was to perform the task well, and with the other, my ambition was to remain committed and not quit. "If you're not feeling brave enough to win, then just don't lose" was a sort of mantra that I would use when I needed to.

On some dark, cold, rainy mornings, the last thing I wanted to do was get out of bed and go into the winter elements wearing nothing but my Lycra tights and a thin long-sleeved shirt. But knowing that my teammates were going to be waiting at the boathouse made it much easier to go. On some days I'd want to head back to the dock early and cut short a practice, but my teammates were still going, so I always kept going too.

For a career champion that "weakness" is just another source of motivation to draw on. I don't care so much where the motivation comes from—I just care that it comes. To avoid having others think less of me, I'll often dig a little deeper or do a little more when facing a challenge.

It was hard as a young athlete to keep that level of accountability when I was training alone. I had to learn to be as accountable to myself as I was to others. The easiest person to let down and disappoint is yourself, so you have to train constantly not to.

DIG DOWN FOR MORE

On the fourth day of the multi-sport adventure race that I did in 2003, I felt more exhausted than I ever had before. I had experienced acute fatigue and pain from a seven-minute, all-out effort in rowing races, but when the Canadian Eco Challenge pushed our team of four to run, climb, rappel, cycle, and paddle through the mountains near Golden, B.C., I felt an overwhelming fatigue that I had never known before.

I clearly recall a cycling portion of the race where I needed to use every tool I had to not quit. Even with all of the commitment and accountability skills that I had developed when rowing, I still needed a huge amount of help from my team. We were on a mountain-biking section that was a logging road following a quick-switchback pattern up the side of a mountain. The road was so steep that even with the repeated hairpin turns to reduce the incline, the climb was intense.

An adventure race team is usually a co-ed group of four people who must work together to cover the course as fast as possible. In canoes, to keep both boats moving along together, the strongest paddler will be paired with the weakest. It would be counterproductive for one boat to be stronger and faster. Not only would the slower boat hold up the faster one, but the team members in the slower boat would be significantly more fatigued by their effort. The same is true when cycling. If one or two of the team members are particularly strong on the bike, then teams will often use a bungee cord to attach a strong cyclist to a weaker one. It was a blow to my Olympic champion ego when my bike was bungeed to Ollie Blake's bike, but he was clearly a stronger cyclist than I was.

Like our teammates Kevin and Paul, whose bikes were also attached, Ollie and I worked together to move up the steep mountain road. The bungee allowed a gap of about twelve inches between Ollie's back tire and my front tire. At first, my commitment to the climb came easily. I was working with Ollie, and the challenge of the road was fun. My eyes were on the bungee that connected us. As I matched Ollie's speed, the gap stayed constant and Ollie didn't have to pull me.

Pedal, pedal, pedal, turn left. Pedal, pedal, pedal, turn right. Pedal, pedal, pedal, left. The road went on and on, and my fatigue grew and my legs became increasingly pain racked. As the challenge to keep pedalling increased, my accountability shifted from the fun of doing it for me to the task of doing it for my team's perception of me. I have always thought of myself as strong and fit. When I wasn't so sure that I could be strong and fit for me, I decided to be strong and fit for my team. The bungee stretched another three inches. The fifteen-inch gap between our tires meant that Ollie was pulling a little more of my load up the hill. But we both kept pedalling.

This new source of accountability worked, but only for so long. Soon it shifted again. As the lactic acid began to reach painful levels in my legs, I wasn't sure that I could be strong and fit for anyone anymore. The bungee had stretched again to an eighteen-inch gap. I knew that Ollie was working hard to pedal himself up the mountain while also pulling me. It had been enough just to think that I didn't want to be seen as a quitter, but that conviction started to fade. I knew that I had been put on the team because I was an Olympic champion. My team believed, like most people, that Olympic champions don't quit. It didn't matter to them that I was an Olympic champion rower, not an adventure racer. Even though I was thinking about quitting, I drew on my ego; I didn't want Ollie to think that an Olympic champion would quit.

My ego provided some extra accountability, but soon I was prepared to let go. My legs were screaming; I felt spent. The negative voices in my head were reminding me that I was a *rowing* champion; clearly no one would expect me to be a cycling champion too. This uphill mountain climb had broken me. I was ready to quit. The gap between Ollie's bike and mine was now about twenty to twenty-four inches. Ollie was working tremendously hard. If I were to stop without giving him any notice, the sudden pull from my end of the cord could cause him to fall off his bike. With great regret I spoke up. "Ollie. I'm done. We've got to stop." He kept pedalling, so I kept pedalling. The bungee stretched some more. Had he heard me? "Ollie! I'm done."

I had given up on me, but apparently Ollie wasn't prepared to give up on himself or us. I will never forget the impact of his reply. As he continued to pedal, he turned and looked me in the eyes; he was obviously working hard. In an almost imploring voice he asked, "Can't I try a little harder? Can't I do a little more for us?" Ollie wasn't asking—he was telling me that he wanted to do more. His commitment to the climb and accountability to the goal were inspiring.

"Can't I do a little more for us?" he had asked. To be clear, Ollie Blake is not a big guy. At five feet ten I was at least three inches taller than him, and with my powerful rower's legs (which, sadly, were no longer helping me on this climb) I probably outweighed him by about thirty pounds. And yet here was this relatively small man *powering* us both up this mountain. I was prepared to let myself down, but no way was I going to let this kind of commitment down. I didn't have much left in my legs to give, but I was motivated again and I gave it.

I had absolutely believed that I was done. I had been prepared to give up but I became accountable to Ollie. I was motivated to keep my legs going for him, and I found some more. I kept pedalling, letting Ollie pull the lion's share. The bungee stretched farther than I thought it could, and yet we continued up, focussing on one switchback section at a time. The light rotations that my legs went through worked to flush some of the toxic lactic acid from my muscles, and soon I was able to contribute more and more. The gap started to decrease again. We made it to the top of the road without stopping, something that I would not have been able to do by myself.

Motivation can be drawn from anywhere. Where you draw it from is less important than the fact that you draw it. If a moment of personal weakness can be averted simply because you are a bit vain and don't want to *look* weak, then bring on vanity! If I find myself lacking drive on a particular day but I'm too proud to be seen being passed, then I will use pride as a motivator.

Accepting that my motivation will come from anywhere allows me to be more flexible. Where I get it from on great days will likely be a different place than on bad days. If the motivation that I had been relying on has escaped me, I simply look for another source. Ego, pride, passion, joy—it doesn't matter. If it helps me pursue more, I'm happy to use it.

SET YOUR GOALS IN STONE

Another way to see your collection of goals is simply as your to-do list. Working on your various goals, some of which feel more like responsibilities (keep the house clean, balance your budget, walk the dog), can force you to juggle your time and ambitions. Whether you can remain strictly focussed on one task and its goal or you need to jump in and out of the pursuit of several, you have to be careful not to lower the bar just to get everything done. Keeping the accountability and commitment you have to each goal takes some work!

Sometimes you are able to deal easily with the challenges of the range of tasks you have going. But these challenges aren't always a test of your preparation. Just because you *can* do something doesn't necessarily mean that you *will* do it (or vice versa). Knowing that you shouldn't eat the fully loaded nachos doesn't always stop you from eating them. But your accountability and commitment can.

Ambition, passion, ego, vanity, perceived expectations, pride—whatever I could tap into to keep me accountable and committed I would use. It's hard to stay accountable all of the time. When everything you are trying to do seems hard, it's easy to get disconnected from what you originally committed to. Allowing yourself to create grey zones between what you wanted to do and didn't want to do is a slippery slope. That is why you need to use whatever tools are at your disposal.

To maximize these tools, it's critical that you care about your goals, and it's equally important that other people are aware of what you want and care about. Making others aware of your goals helps you keep them from slipping back into the just-a-dream category. Other people can be a very powerful tool in motivating you. They can dramatically increase your chances of staying accountable, committed, and motivated. They don't even have to do anything; sometimes they just have to know.

Making the right decision and acting on it will come from your accountability. When you keep your goals to yourself, you write them in chalk. If you tell a friend, a teammate, your family, or even the media about your goals, then it is as if you have carved them in stone. You become firmly bound to the goals.

Challenges test your commitment to a goal and make you wonder, "Can I?" or "Will I?" Do I have to keep pushing so hard? Are the little details really important to me? A strong commitment to your goal will compel you to push harder to see it through. That commitment is reinforced if the goal is set in stone.

If your goal is in chalk, then the easy way to manage the "Can I? Will I?" questions is to simply erase the goal and rewrite. Losing twenty-five pounds becomes a fifteen-pound target; winning turns into finishing in the top three. As the task continues to challenge you, with no hard commitment, you can adjust the goal down again: five pounds, top eight. The only person you are disappointing is the only person who knew what the goal was—and that's yourself.

Even for those who perform as individuals, staying committed to a goal can be greatly supported by a team effort. When you question your commitment and accountability and consider easing the target, you are far less likely to do so if you feel that you will let someone else down. Your team will rarely know that it is involved in your decision making; it's not about their task and performance but about your own.

At my first World Championships, in 1989, we were extremely happy to finish fourth in the four. Often fourth is referred to as the worst place for an athlete to finish, since it is just outside of the medals. But we were young and racing at our first Worlds. It had been very exciting.

As exciting as it was, fourth left us hungry for more. We were so close to the podium, we could practically taste it.

With all that fire and another year of solid training, we were keen to start the next World Cup season. In the summer races of 1990, the East Germans and Romanians were the class of the field, but we beat the West Germans and the Americans, which meant that we had a great shot at the World Championship podium that year.

In my head I worked out all of the possibilities. With a great race we could win the bronze medal. My teammates—Kathleen, Kirsten, and Brenda—did the same calculations. We had done everything we could all year to prepare to be on the podium except tell each other *exactly* what we believed we could do in this final. We remained vague, saying things like "We could do something *special* this year." But we never said exactly what "special" meant. Looking back, I think we were afraid to say, "We should be third," because the podium was still foreign to us. When it mattered, it was as if we were afraid to go for it—we lacked the accountability to each other to risk it.

We rowed the final race of that year into an incredible headwind. Halfway through the race we were in third place, where we expected to be, but the wind was punishing. The West Germans were in fourth, close beside us. We could sense that they were starting to make a move to pass. To respond to the West Germans' burst of speed, we would have had to find something extra. We didn't. We simply didn't respond. We didn't do anything less, but we didn't do anything more. We remained accountable and committed to our race plan, but we had failed to create any accountability to our goal—to be third. For the second year in a row, we were fourth; this time the bitter dramatically overpowered the sweet.

After the race, we all agreed that we were disappointed because we knew that we had the potential to beat the West Germans. But there was more. We were all disappointed because we all had felt that there had been a moment when we should have attacked. We discussed what had gone through our mind during the race. Phrases like "We're in the World Championship final" and "Doing everything we planned" were unfortunately common. We had needed a great race and it seemed that we had settled into just a good one.

Our goal to win a medal had been written in chalk; we had left it as vague, so we had a vague commitment to it. If we had had the guts to say to each other that we believed we could be third, that we could beat the West Germans at the Worlds, our goal would have been carved in stone. That understanding and commitment to each other could have ignited a rally to push harder. Had the words in our minds been "Go for it," "Stay ahead," or "You can beat them," there is no telling if we would actually have come in third—but I wouldn't be writing about that race as one I regret.

From then on we wouldn't be afraid to articulate to each other what our specific goals were. If we wanted to do something bold, then we had to be brave enough to say something bold. There would be no more backing off on a goal because we hadn't been clear about the target.

That commitment got put to the test the very next year when I started racing the pair with Kathleen Heddle. We were at the Lucerne regatta, the most important World Cup race of the year. Our training had gone extremely well, and our early races indicated that we were capable of doing something "really special." In our semifinal, which had been unfairly packed with more of the world's top-ranked crews than the other, we had beaten everyone. We knew we needed to say it out loud. It was a surprisingly scary thing to say, but I remember the first time I looked at Kathleen and said, "I think we can win the final." My heart and mind raced with the audacity of the statement. "Me too" was her simple reply. It was all we needed. We made clear what we expected of me and her and us. We set it in stone; we believed that we could be champions. Our accountability to that goal was fixed. It was a goal that we achieved—our first World Cup win, with many more to follow.

YOU HAVE TO KNOW WHY

Using the team around you, whether they are partners in the performance or your support team, can help remind you that you really want something. You can sometimes forget that you *chose* your really challenging goals. Your team members can help keep you connected to your accountability, but they can't do it alone. Just as ambition is a multiplier and can affect accountability and commitment only if you have some, your team can help keep you accountable only if you (and they) know why it's important to you.

Knowing what you want to do—what your goal is—is essential to give you direction. Remembering why you want it is going to be the key that gets you past all the doubts and fears. When you question your own accountability and commitment, knowing where your ambition comes from with absolute certainty makes decision making easy. Knowing who you want to be will direct you to what you believe to be important and why. How you define yourself (and want to define yourself in the future) can give clues that will help you to support and understand your decision making.

In 2009, the Canadian Olympic Committee held a meeting for athletes and their support who were going to the Vancouver 2010 Olympic Games. At a session titled "My Team Is...," there were over two hundred people representing the spectrum of winter sports, from freestyle skiing to curling.

Team sports like hockey and short-track speed skating, endurance sports like Nordic skiing and long-track speed skating, and finesse sports like figure skating and curling were all represented. All of the sport teams were brought together as a "capital T" team: the Canadian Team.

Although a freestyle skier would never be involved in the performance of a figure skater, we felt that the sense of belonging to the Canadian Team could be empowering. All of these athletes could share the weight of the expectations of the nation and the unique stresses of an Olympic stage. Feeling part of the larger Canadian Team, rather than just their own sport team, could boost each athlete's positive inner voice.

Many were meeting for the first time and wouldn't see each other again until they gathered to compete at the Olympic Games. Still, in less than a year they would be a team. There wouldn't be any significant time to bond, so we needed to provide the group with a tool or icon that would remind them why this team was important to them. Once they knew why it was important, they could tap into their commitment and accountability to this larger team.

We chose to have them define who they wanted to be together. I asked them, "When you walk into the Olympic Stadium, how do you want people to see you, as a team? How do you want Canadians to think of you—and this team? What do you want your competitors and teammates to think of you?" Working in small groups, the team came up with words that, for them, answered the questions.

passionate	determined	enthusiastic
unbreakable	respectful	winners
alive	honourable	accountable

dynamic	fun	sexy
admirable	present	focussed
confident	fearless	intimidating
ready	hungry	gracious
ethical	leaders	united
resilient	professional	unforgettable
tenacious		

After collecting all the words that the team felt could represent who they wanted to be, we said we'd be asking each athlete to pick his or her top five. These words would reinforce their accountability and commitment to who they wanted to be and the type of team they wanted to be on and why. Each athlete was given five dot stickers; they marked their choices and left for lunch.

We counted the votes and found *confident, ready, sexy, passionate, resilient,* and *united* were the clear favourites. I have to admit I was surprised by *sexy,* but who was I to define who this group wanted to be? In part, I supposed, *sexy* was just about having fun and feeling good about themselves.

The next step was to put these words into stone for the group. We began to fill in "My Team is... /*Mon Équipe est...*" posters with their chosen words. These posters would be signed by everyone and would hang in the Canadian parts of the Olympic Village to remind them of their commitment.

Just as we were about to commit the words to the poster, one of the short-track speed skating athletes approached me. He seemed excited to hear that his favourite word had made the list, but then he got a bit bashful. He admitted that he "may" have stuffed the ballot box a bit for *sexy*. In fact, he admitted to using extra dot stickers and voting over twenty times for it! I laughed so hard.

Confident, ready, passionate, resilient, and *united* were the powerful words that this 2010 Canadian Olympic Team committed to. (*Sexy* was no longer a clear group favourite and was dropped from the list. Although they may have been a sexy group, that was not a word that was going to define their training and preparation.) That group became a team because they were united in their commitment and accountability to how they wanted to compete and who they wanted to be.

During the 2010 Olympic Games, the Canadian flag-bearer, Clara Hughes, spoke *passionately* about what sport had given her and her peers: an opportunity to live better, healthier lives. Each team member, whether an athlete or a support member, was incredibly prepared and *confident.* The fourteen gold medals that they won were more than any country had ever won at a Winter Olympics and proved that they had been *ready.* The whole team was proudly *united* by the uniform. The dreams and goals they shared inspired Canadians from coast to coast. Joannie Rochette epitomized *resilience* when she skated in her mother's honour and won a bronze medal just days after her mother had died of a heart attack. This team had defined themselves well.

The athletes of the 2008 Canadian Olympic Team had chosen these words to represent them: *professional, tenacious, united, genuinely respectful,* and *supportive.* Four years later, the words on the newest "My Team Is..." list include *proud, unbreakable, world class, fierce,* and *relentless.* This new list bodes well for the team's goal to advance from the top sixteen nations in Beijing to the top twelve in London. Their words have moved from being supportive in nature to radiating confidence and strength.

Who do *you* want to be and why is that important? As individuals, we often take ourselves for granted. We assume that we know ourselves completely, so we rarely take much notice of ourselves. We know we want things. We know what our goals are. But do we know *why?*

Finding who we want to be is another item on our to-do list; it's our ultimate goal. Right now I may see myself as thoughtful, fair, hard-working, confident, and happy. Some of these words mean many things to me, but I think they are fairly accurate. Perhaps when I was competing, I would have used different, stronger words.

These words help me with my accountability and commitment to the goals that I've set for myself—the ones I've started, and the ones I'm hoping to get to. My obligation to myself to be who I've committed to be will determine whether I act on my goals. Whether I have put my goals in stone or left them in chalk will also play a part. Since I have written the words down here, in *The Power of More,* I wrap every reader of this book in my accountability to them. They are in stone now.

6

ACTION:

The Test

THE test for an athlete comes in his or her performance at a competition. The Olympic motto *"Citius, Altius, Fortius"* (Faster, Higher, Stronger) describes how an athlete will be measured. Performance in sport is easy to gauge. Team selection and other competitions are usually defined by clear, objective standards; athletes know when and how they will be tested. A healthy mind is an asset, but the strength and abilities of their bodies will often be the key to their success. The beginning of the performance is clearly defined, and the end will produce winners and losers.

Performance success or ranking outside of sport isn't always as obvious. If the start and finish aren't clear, how are most people judged? When will they be tested? How does a nurse, contractor, or teacher know if he or she is among the best? For many of your goals, your success will be evaluated according to a question, not an action: "Is your product right for me?" "Do you know...?" "Can you help?" These questions that can make or break you can come at any time. Presentations and reports are really just long, detailed answers to a question or a series of questions. The value of your persistent efforts to fill your cup with grains of rice will show at this time.

We judge competence, our own and that of others, by the ability to answer questions and solve problems. Competitions don't exist to determine the best contractor, teacher, doctor, lawyer, or even parents, but we often determine their level of skill by the quality of their answers and the thoroughness of their knowledge. "Can you build a house under these guidelines and restrictions?" "Can you manage a classroom and inspire learning by the whole class?" "Can you remain calm when faced with an epidemic of disease?" "Can you protect my estate from paying unnecessary taxes?" It's an athlete's body that is trained and eventually tested; others are tested by how they have trained and prepared their minds.

The mind and the body work together. As much as I needed to work and prepare my body to achieve more, when it came time to perform I was a better competitor when my mind was also reaching for more. Similarly, success outside of physical performance comes more consistently to those who have prepared themselves intellectually while maintaining a healthy body.

RESPECT COMES BEFORE FRIENDSHIP

I've heard it said that you choose your friends but you can't choose your family. That could be why people also say that you have to love your family but you don't have to like them. The same can be said of teammates and the people you work with.

It is rare in a performance environment that we get to choose our teammates or co-workers. More often, we are assigned to them. In a working environment, we are grouped by our abilities, not by our likes and dislikes. Although our co-workers are often around us for a far greater percentage of our day than the people we choose, we must remember that it is not our job to make these people our friends. It would be very nice and would make life way easier if we all liked each other, but in pursuit of more, respect is what we need.

Our resolve to stay committed and accountable to the dream will be tested, which is why we need to surround ourselves with people whom we respect. We need to be able to rely on their advice, support, and direction. The value of respect cannot be overstated.

I had a coach once who made the mistake of trying too hard to be our friend. What we needed and wanted was a leader we respected who would push us to improve. Before she was assigned to coach our crew, we were a group of single scullers working well together; we had to think for ourselves. Our commitment and accountability were very high, and we were strict with each other. There was a tremendous amount of respect.

We took turns demanding more from each other—being the bitch on board. We asked as much from each other as we did from ourselves. Punctual, focussed, and prepared to take initiative as required, we were proud of the results of our training. We were friendly and supportive with each other, but on the water our priority was respect, which isn't always kind.

We were excited that a coach was finally assigned to work with us. Unfortunately, things didn't go as we hoped. Our accountability and commitment seemed to drain away from us the more our new coach offered to pitch in. Her best intentions to help with some of the simple things that we had been taking care of did nothing but make us lazy and reliant on her. She was kind and liked to chat, but our workouts began starting later and later. With soft-target meeting times instead of the strict ones that we had set, we tended to show up late to our on-water meeting points. Even though this meant the group would have to wait to start, there were no repercussions.

The proverbial last straw came when she started making our workouts easier for us. From the coach boat she saw us working hard and began to empathize with us. If a workout included six very hard eight-minute pieces, she started to "reward" our efforts and cut the workout down to five. We had worked so hard to make the effort of giving more our norm, but in trying to be our friend, she was helping us accept less. This didn't help us achieve our goal of greatness.

We stopped looking after ourselves and expected someone else to do it for us. We were not being efficient or respectful with our time. We weren't getting what we actually wanted: someone who would be as accountable to our carved-in-stone goals as we were. The goal wasn't to be pushed and coddled onto the podium but to learn how to climb on and stay there. We didn't need a friend; we needed a leader.

The coaches who lowered the bar for me are very nice people, but they lost my respect. I've had some coaches who have pushed me extremely hard, and I have even liked some of them! More importantly, I respected all of them because they set a hard target to achieve and then helped me reach for it. Al Morrow, who was the most influential coach in my career, never tried to be my friend. He tried to be my coach, and as a result I gained great respect for him. Even without trying, we became friends.

With our peers, our leaders, or those we lead, our role is to earn their respect. If we are lucky, we will also become friends.

NOBODY TRAINS TO WAIT

On an Olympic start line, if I look over my shoulder, I can see the finish 2,000 metres away. There is no way for me to get there but to row there.

My whole Olympic journey started with a dream to win an Olympic gold medal. (Okay—I confess that dancing and partying at the Closing Ceremony may have been the original reason, but once I actually picked a sport and got near the national team, Olympic gold it was!) Initially, the gap between those two moments—dreaming of gold at the start line and crossing the finish line first—was massive and I had no idea how to bridge it. Thankfully, I have spent years working on my task, and nothing helps fill a gap better than focussing on the task at hand.

Even with the best plan, the best preparation, and an enormous amount of motivation, nothing is done until it's actually done. Medals don't get mailed out to people who are ready to win. Task, and task alone, gets you where you want to go. Long before my team got to the Olympics or the World Championships or even a World Cup race, we had been taught to focus on our task. Everything that we had been doing, the collection of all those grains of rice, was simply so that we could row as well as possible. Simply put, our task was to row; good rowing makes you go fast, and going really fast gets you to the finish line first, which wins gold medals.

For some challenges, someone else will start you going, often at a set time, and for others, you have to start yourself— whenever you choose. With the first, you will start whether you are ready or not; with the second, you begin performing whenever you are ready. There is advantage and disadvantage to both. Which is harder—starting or waiting to start? For some, the delayed moment before we cold-call someone who isn't expecting to hear from us, before we knock on a door, or before we press Send can be so extended that the call, the visit, or the transmission of the email never happens.

Quiet as they might seem, the moments before the start can be nerve-racking. You can guess, but you don't know exactly how things are going to go until you start. The best thing to do for those nerves is start. There is a calm in the actual task no matter how furious its pace. We train and prepare to *do;* we don't train to wait. If you have created a goal-achieving plan, then act on the plan. If you want to start an exercise program or stop smoking or go on a diet, don't wait for Monday, or January 1; do it now. The hardest part of the task might be just starting it.

The calm that is observed before storms can also occur before big races. It's not really a calm as much as it is a shifting of pressure and wind direction from one extreme to another, from preparation to performance. There is nothing more to do—all the energy that has been accumulated is about to be released. That calm always freaked me out. The most stressful part of every big race that I had was waiting for the race to begin. That time before you start is when negative thoughts fill that quiet space and threaten to derail your best-laid plans and goals. Experience and preparation allow a champion to expect all of those thoughts and just let them drift on by.

When the action finally starts, there is no anxiety; I am too busy working. I have trained for that moment. Just seconds before, my mind would have been racing with possibilities, but the race is about action. I am still stressed because I care deeply about what and how I am doing, but in the performance of the task I am calm.

I remember reading that actors, just before the curtain goes up, often feel panic and worry that they have forgotten all of their lines. I often felt the same way as I approached the start gates. When I turned to look down my 2,000-metre lane, I was completely unsure whether I could make it that far. That distance would take approximately 220 to 240 strokes, but in my warm-up I felt I was physically struggling to do only twenty. Not surprisingly, once the race started, I never worried about making it to the finish line. From that moment I would focus only on making it to the finish fast.

RACE ACCORDING TO YOUR PLAN

When an opportunity to be tested comes, regardless of the opposition or conditions, you have to be ready to act. Expecting to be overmatched can throw you off your game plan, just as expecting too little can. I heard a world champion 1,500-metre runner comment that it was as shocking for her to be leading the pack as it had been in other races when she had fallen dramatically behind. To win her race, she had remained focussed on her own race plan. This is why it's important to have a good idea of what your game plan is.

A good race plan is structured like most business presentations or sales pitches. A race plan is created to maximize effectiveness and speed. It takes advantage of all of one's strengths while weaving support around weaknesses, which cannot be ignored. It should start with a bang to establish authority and finish with a flourish to answer any unfinished business. Although you might have to adjust your plan to fit the situation, you don't want to lose your strengths while adjusting to the strengths or weaknesses of others.

"Never argue with an idiot. They will drag you down to their level and win with experience" is a quip that I think epitomizes that idea. If you pace yourself only by others, they may hold you back or even pull down your performance. Professional sport teams in Toronto don't have the best track record, but Torontonians love to hope and dream anyway. When the National Basketball Association brought a team to Toronto, many hoped that the Raptors would bring the success that the Maple Leafs had missed for so long in hockey. There was an excited buzz in the city once when the Raptors beat the legendary Michael Jordan and his Chicago Bulls. The hopeful question "Could this possibly be the year?" was quickly answered when the last-place Vancouver Grizzlies beat the Toronto team the next day. The Raptors had lifted their game for one opponent and dropped it for another. (For Toronto's professional sports, you have to go way back for even glimmers of hope!)

Basing your assessment of your own abilities on mistaken judgments about how you stack up against your opponents or training partners can affect your confidence in your preparation. If you undervalue your training partners or your own past accomplishments, you could find yourself discouraged before you even start your next competition. The opposite is also true, and more dangerous. When you get a chance to broaden your competition experience, you can be shocked to discover that the real quality of your home league was much lower than you gave them (and yourself) credit for. So while it is essential to feel that you are prepared, more often than not, you won't know that you are ready until you are actually tested.

I went to a race in Germany where I was quite sure that I would be lucky to manage a mediocre result in the single. I had been training in Victoria with and against other

Canadians who I knew were good, but I still assumed that the level of international racing would humble me. In the race, I put my head down and focussed on my task, and to my surprise, I won. It turned out that the quality of my little training group was extremely high. I had no idea until I stepped out of our little fishbowl.

It's a difficult thing to go into a competition blind. To have no idea how your preparation is going to stand up against the preparation of others is extremely stressful. It would be really nice to have a string of successes to provide confidence, but where does that success start? In the beginning, you just have to trust that your preparation cup is as full as you could have made it.

At the conclusion of every competitive season, we would return home and begin training so that we would go faster the next year. Our competitors did exactly the same thing. Often we were the ones with a target on our back; our competitors looked to us like the crew to beat. That was their advantage; everyone chasing the champion has a clear idea of whom they need to beat. They can see the gap they need to close. Being the target makes the goal harder to identify. Our ambitious new standard had to be imagined.

Preparing for the next season meant continuing to do and redo what was going well for us: lifting weights, rowing countless kilometres, and drilling our technique constantly. It also meant adding new ideas and embracing new concepts. Last year's plan is just that until it is tweaked and becomes new. And so we always embraced something new, and new almost always means more. Raise the bar, improve the quality and speed of our fishbowl—no matter how we phrased it, we had to continually add as many grains of rice to our cup as we could and hope that we would be faster for our efforts.

LEARN TO PUSH YOURSELF

Each year, before the Canadian rowing team travelled to Europe, a time trial was held to prove that we were fast enough to be sent to World Cup racing. It was a pre-emptive test of the quality of our fishbowl. Even though each boat would race 2,000 metres, single file, and against a clock, we were all keenly aware that we were racing against each other. The team has only one boat in each category, so Kathleen and I, in the double, would have to race in the trials against our men's eight, a light women's double, or a women's quad—which, considering that a men's eight goes about two minutes faster than a women's double, hardly seems fair. A percentage-based scoring method based on each event's world's-best time allowed for a women's double with a world's-best time of 6 minutes, 38 seconds to fairly compare against a men's eight whose world's-best time was 5 minutes, 19 seconds.

In contrast to a normal six-boat competition, this single-file style of racing is a very quiet and lonely way to race. One boat is sent off every twenty seconds, and the order is set so that you are unlikely to pass or be passed. There is no antagonist beside you, no opponent to react to or push against. There is no way of knowing if you are going fast or not. If this race were in a fishbowl, there would be only one fish. For a spectator, it would be as exciting as watching a single horse run laps of a track. For the rowers, however, every second counts.

Even though an Olympic final is stressful, I can tell you that time trials and the first race of the season, to me, were the most nerve-racking. After almost eight months of preparation, all we had was a gut feeling that we were fast. You can take your numbers and statistics and make them mean anything you want. You can build yourself up: you're fast, your product is great; or you can take yourself down: you have some problems, you're slow. But until you actually go head to head, all you have is an idea that what happens in your fishbowl is pretty good.

How do we push for more? More than whom? It had to be about us, our race plan, our sense of performance. I believe the time-trial challenge, along with other tests like it, is where we developed our international reputation for performance on demand. Those isolated trials taught us to demand more from ourselves and showed us very fast results when we did. We didn't need the presence of others to make us go fast or want to go even faster. It showed us how to race our own race regardless of the field we were competing in. Even if we hadn't had a race in a long time, getting all the thoughts of other people and how they were going to race out of our head gave us the confidence to just trust ourselves and go.

The first time we arrived at a World Cup regatta, with just enough ego to think that we could win, was terrifying. Even though our training and time-trial results had been excellent, we had no swagger. To make things worse, our first race seemed stacked. Four of the six finalists from the previous World Championship finals were in our race, including the world champions and the bronze medallist.

All we had was a sense that we were fast, but we had no idea if we were *that* fast. We knew nothing about the tactics of the other crews, and we had no idea how our race strategy would hold up against theirs. We avoided trying to imagine what the other crews would do. We would unleash the fastest race we could and see how it would hold up. We tapped into something we were familiar with and called it our time-trial approach.

Racing with a time-trial strategy allowed us the freedom to let go of our worries about our opponents and see what abilities we had. As a season would progress, we would incorporate some of the other teams' tactics into our plan, but for the most part, we determined that we always performed better when we pushed ourselves and raced our own race.

FOCUS ON THE HARD PARTS FIRST

Although I have been a world and Olympic champion six times, I never trained to be a world or Olympic champion. I trained to row better and faster than anyone else. More specifically, I trained to stay balanced, put my blade in the water, and pull it as hard as I could while following my teammates. I get more peace of mind from that focus than from thinking about winning races.

I appreciate all of my medals and I'm happy to have them, but dreaming about standing on a podium with a hunk of metal hanging from a ribbon did nothing to help me get from the start line to the finish line. Even when I did mental imagery —a technique used by many athletes and performers to envision a desired outcome—before a race, I learned to put my task first.

Before Kathleen and I would race, I would talk us through our on-water warm-up, describing what conditions we could expect, where our competitors would be, and how tense we would feel in the start gate. Together we would mentally rehearse our strategy and expectations for the race. Even though I would discuss the race profile and tactics that we expected from our opponents, at this point we never mentioned results. Our pre-race imagery was 100 per cent about the task.

Throughout the year I would let myself dream. My personal imagery was very similar to that of my pre-race routine with Kathleen, but I included the luxury of the medal ceremony. At first I found myself dreaming *only* about the medal ceremony. Everything was perfect, the sky was always blue, the wind and water were always calm. We would be the heroes; my teammates and I would be beaming as we waved to the cheering crowd.

Then I realized I was letting myself enjoy all the glory of the goal with none of the effort of the task; I wasn't earning it. At first I found it very difficult to shift my imagery to focus more on the race. My mind would try to skip ahead to the fun bits because doing 220 strokes in my brain was boring.

To make the imagery interesting, I made it harder. We made mistakes. The conditions were never perfect; I created races in rain, wind, and scorching heat. We never got an early or easy lead, and if we did, another crew would fight back to challenge us. Every stroke in my mind became a ferocious battle, so much so that often, even in my imagery, I was practically gasping for air when I finally got onto the podium. Creating some soul-testing situations to overcome in 220 strokes became a favourite game.

If what you are preparing for is going to come in the form of a question, what is the hardest set of questions that could come? Layer onto that some situations that could make the moment even more challenging. Playing the "What if?" game not only allows you to anticipate what to prepare for, it allows you to imagine and "see" how you will handle the situation when it comes. What if your car broke down and you were on your way to a presentation? What if you were sick on an important interview day? What if your biggest competitor were allowed to sit in and watch your presentation? What would you say if you met the "right" person in an elevator?

As I improved my ability to picture difficult races, I realized that I no longer had any patience for the medal ceremony. It was more fun playing "What if?" Although that hero moment on the podium had originally been my dream, it was the act of performing my task really well that had become my goal.

"CAN I? WILL I?"

The path to achieve our goals will challenge us. Although we should also have some goals that are fairly easy to achieve, we should fill our lives with things that provide some challenge. Actually, we tend to choose those goals *because* they challenge us. They are the fun ones. Having an ambition that stresses and pushes us for more makes life more interesting.

When it gets hard, we question our accountability, our commitment, and the very thing that we are motivated to achieve. The question we ask ourselves when we are challenged is "Can I do this?" And, more importantly, "Will I do this?"

"Can I? Will I?" moments occur regularly. Sometimes the answer comes easily. But just because you can do something doesn't mean you will (or should). I can sing, but no way am I going to. It doesn't take much for me to make a decision about this, since it's not a task that I feel any commitment to.

Training with the national team regularly included workouts that were designed to be very difficult. Almost every day I would run into at least one "Can I? Will I?" moment. In contrast to the question about singing, the workout question was often very difficult to answer. The exhausting amount of training tempted me to say no. But I had trained too much to stop and had too much ambition to do anything but try.

A response to a "Can I? Will I?" moment may require a physical action or a verbal one. Sometimes when a question is posed in a meeting, no one responds. It may be that people have an answer but lack courage to offer it up. Maybe they think they can answer, but will they risk being wrong? When your task is challenging and you ask, "Can I? Will I?" you have three choices. Which one you pick will be decided by your ambition as well as your commitment and accountability to all of the preparation that you've put toward your goal.

The first choice when things get hard is to quit. If you lack accountability to your goal—if it's in chalk—you can give yourself permission to stop chasing it. Maybe you even decide it was never really your goal in the first place. It's a bad day and you just want out. If you quit once, you are cracked. If you quit twice, you risk being broken. Like any good habit that we repeat over and over while trying to learn, quitting can become a pattern. Quitting becomes easier the more we do it. We learn to allow it, then to expect it.

Maybe we have to quit once to learn the lesson never to quit again. I know I did. In my very first year of rowing I was given the opportunity to try out for the junior national rowing team. I was told that I had to do a test on a rowing ergometer. I'd never done anything so hard, and it felt so long. As my body struggled, my mind started looking for ways out. Who was I to think that I could try out for a national rowing team? I was a nobody.

So I stopped. Just over four minutes into the six-minute test, I quit. The machine went quiet all of a sudden, and everyone in the lab looked over. I was thinking about what I'd just done. Had I really just quit? I had only about two minutes remaining. Then I got really angry with myself; I'm no quitter! Furious, I started again and redoubled my efforts. Even with the stop in the middle, I completed the test with not a bad score. I was so disappointed in myself. Imagine what I could have done if I hadn't stopped! I made the team, but I never forgave myself for quitting. I hated how it felt to stop for even that brief moment. I hated wondering how I would have done. I learned that quitting is an option that should be avoided.

Although the second choice is a better option, it is not the preferred choice of a career champion. When facing a "Can I? Will I?" moment, some people choose to close their eyes and pray.

Before the 2001 World Triathlon Championships, I told this to a group of participants, and one of them spoke out to challenge my suggestion that this second choice was a poor option. As it turned out, seventy-year-old Sister Madonna Buder, a very successful triathlete in her age group, prays all the time. (At age eighty, Sister Madonna, known as the Iron Nun, has now run over 350 triathlons.) Still, I doubt that sunbeams or angels appeared to make any of her triathlon "Can I? Will I?" moments go away. In sport, only the athlete can do that. Sister Madonna trained extremely hard so that her prayers would work that well.

To be more precise, the second choice involves doing no more and no less than what you are currently doing. It doesn't mean that you give up, but it doesn't require you to try harder. It encompasses letting go of accountability and letting the situation move to wherever it will organically go. We watch the clock tick or the calendar page turn; somehow this moment, this day, this term will end. But with eyes closed and hands off the steering wheel, the performer relinquishes control of the direction and outcome. This second choice involves hoping for luck and flukes. Although you may have worked hard enough to be lucky and know that flukes count, there is no controlling them.

The problem with this choice is that at the end of the day you are left with a deep sense of "what if?" What if I had done something more or tried for just a little longer? Those thoughts linger with us. We don't always get second chances, but a memory of regret can last for a long, long time.

The third choice is to attack. At the moment that you begin to question yourself, you attack your doubts and push into the unknown. I shared the concept of the three choices with the Canadian speed skating team in 2005. A remarkable group of athletes, they would go on to win eight medals at the 2006 Turin Olympics. I was incredibly proud when their coach told me that some of my ideas had had a strong impact. What I found more flattering was how they took my ideas and built on them. Kristina Groves explained that the idea of the three choices had helped her to put some context to the difference between races that she had been happy with and ones she hadn't. In races she was unhappy with, she felt as if she had been waiting for the finish line to come to her. Those were her "close your eyes and pray" races. In the races that she was pleased with, regardless of the outcome, she knew that she had pushed to the finish line.

When our big "Can I? Will I?" moment arrives, if we fold and do not attack, we make all of our preparations meaning-less. Choosing to attack and to push forward doesn't mean that we are assured of the final answer or outcome we want, but it means that, at the very least, we are willing to try. We like to hope that all of our training and learning will encour-age us, when we encounter "Can I? Will I?" questions, to say yes and attack the challenge and push into the unknown. It is the choice of career champions.

"Can I? Will I?" moments aren't all big or obvious. Decid-ing to be punctual, choosing to eat well, or attending class can require effort and decision making. In the end, all we hope for is that we went for it. Winning and being successful is a very cool perk. It often feels like a raison d'être, but we can't con-trol winning; we may put in a stellar effort just when someone else has given the performance of a lifetime. The path that we have followed should stand on its own as a valuable accomplishment, regardless of our final result.

How you respond when you are challenged is where you find respect—for yourself and from others. No one likes to fail; letting yourself or others down is uncomfortable. What you are willing to risk weighs on you at those moments, but simply by accepting the risk of failure you learn more about yourself and the depth of your ambitions. Being willing to risk failure is often a result of being hungry for success.

What you have done and accomplished in the past is yours; it is part of who you are. It is the foundation that supports you and makes you capable of trying, of taking a risk; it is all the rice in your cup.

Some people mistakenly consider their foundation a weight to bear rather than a support. Imagine if all of my training and preparation were put into the form of a pyramid. At the Olympic Games I always felt I was standing on top of that pyramid, held up and empowered by the volume of my experiences and support. For others, it seems that just the opposite occurs. I've seen athletes at the most important moments of their careers feeling oppressed by everything they have done. Mistakenly, they fear that failure now will devalue everything they have done before. Instead of standing at the top, they feel that they are on the bottom and their pyramid is weighing down on them. All of the grains of rice that they have accumulated become a burden instead of an asset. These people hesitate to risk much at a "Can I? Will I?" moment for fear that their whole journey will be judged a waste. Instead of giving 100 per cent, they hold something back. This provides a self-fulfilling excuse for failure. "Well, I would have done it, but..."

You can fail at a given performance, but you do not risk who you are, what you know, and what you can do. There is risk, but the champion's choice is still to attack.

TAKE COMFORT IN YOUR RACE PLAN

No matter how good I got, some things, like the positive and negative voices, never changed. No matter how much I learned and prepared, no matter how experienced I became, those voices stayed with me. I don't want to come across as crazy, but even their messages, though increasingly technical as I improved, stayed the same.

What went through my mind in my last race was very similar to what I'd heard in my first one. The same message has resonated during all the triathlons, half-marathons, and adventure races that I've done. I hear it hiking, biking, snow-shoeing, cross-country skiing. I've even heard it while I was writing this book. It's like an old camp song: "Eighth verse, same as the first. Little bit louder, little bit worse."

The year that I learned to row, I raced in a coxed four. I had just taken a learn-to-row clinic at the Argonaut Rowing Club in Toronto but was surprised that after the two-month clinic I was not selected to the club's top eight. Apparently I still lacked experience (and skill!). The four of us were strong and very keen to improve. Since we didn't have a coach assigned to us, we put it out to the whole club that we were open to any tips and random acts of coaching.

One such random act came at our first regatta. We were inexperienced and had no idea what to expect from racing. All we knew was that it was a 2,000-metre race and there would be five other boats in the race. Before the race, as we took our boat to the dock, one of the other Argos asked, "What's your race plan?" Race plan? I'd never heard the term. We didn't have a race plan. He had some pity for us and took a moment to give us a bit of pre-race coaching. He gave us something to think about after each quarter of the race.

At 500 metres (after the first quarter), he said, your body will be telling you to stop. When your lungs and your legs start screaming, that's okay; just keep going. After 1,000 metres (after the second quarter), your mind will start giving you reasons to stop. When you start telling yourself that you haven't paced yourself well, that you've gone too hard and if you don't ease up you'll never make it, that will be normal, he said. Just keep going. Then, at the 1,500-metre mark (going into the last quarter), your body and your mind will gang up. They will remind you of every blister, sprained ankle, and sore throat that you've had in the last month, trying to convince you to ease up or stop. When your mind and body tell you that you can't, just keep going, because that is normal too. You'll get to the finish line before you know it.

Three markers: our big coaching tip of the season was just three simple markers for the whole 2,000-metre race. Great. But it turned out that those three markers were totally accurate. As I raced, I hit (heard!) them all. At 500 metres, when my legs started to burn, I was oddly comforted. I'd been told to expect that to happen, so when it did I just kept going. At 1,000 metres we were actually winning the race, but my mind was telling me that I shouldn't be winning my very first race and therefore I must be racing too hard and too fast. Then I remembered: it was normal for my brain to doubt at the halfway mark. So I just kept going hard. After 1,500 metres, there they were—my brain and my body ganging up on me. Instead of being intimidated and easing off, I was comforted. I had anticipated this and chose to attack the last 500 metres anyway. Unbelievably, against some very experienced club crews, we did win our very first race. I don't think we would have without our "race plan."

As I learned more about rowing and racing, I developed an increasingly complex race plan. I went from those three original markers to fifteen or twenty markers within a race; I turned "Just keep going" into "Go harder." The original race plan with its simple markers was long forgotten, or so I thought, until I was preparing a crew of novice university rowers for their first race.

What could I say to these young rowers that would be appropriate for their experience level? My race plan would be far too complicated for them. The last thing I wanted to do, right before a race, was add to their stress. From the depths of my memory I dragged up my first race plan. It had been almost seven years since I'd thought about them, but the concept of those three markers came back easily.

Shortly after passing on my advice to the novice rowers, I had a race of my own. As always, the positive and negative voices in my head were with me. As I progressed through my detailed race plan I was shocked to realize that I was still hitting those three markers. My body after the first quarter, my mind at the half, and my mind/body going into the final quarter were still the source of doubts. I had grown so accustomed to anticipating and attacking these issues that I had thought they no longer existed.

To this day, the three markers resonate with me, in every sport and activity that I do, at whatever intensity level. I am still comforted by them. Planning for them is at the core of every performance plan that I make. My Olympic race plans may all have been very complex in comparison, but at their base they are essentially the same. It's been my experience, as

I share these three markers with other people, that they apply almost universally. To create our race or action plans, all we need to know is that much of what we are going to be feeling and thinking, positive and negative, is normal. Then we create a plan that will deal with that and ... just keep going.

EXPECT TO FEEL OFF BALANCE

The point of all of our training and practice is to improve; critical analysis must be constant. This is true not just in sport but in business, sales, artistic performances, and even our relationships. We want to know how we are doing so that we can adjust and correct, so that we can do and give and get more. Athletes and performers can be relentlessly critical during their training, but it doesn't stop there. They tend to be just as critical of their performance, regardless of their result. If you ask athletes right after their competition how they did, they will probably be able to give you a list of things, however obvious or minute, that they would like to have done better. It was rare that I'd finish a race without saying one if not both of the following: "I wish I'd been more aggressive in this section" or "I wish I'd been more technically accurate in that section."

At the start of 1994, there were two internationally ranked single scullers in Canada, Silken Laumann and me. Unfortunately, in rowing, countries can have only one entry per event at the World Championships. A five-race series was agreed upon to choose the top Canadian: the Canadian small-boat rowing championships and four World Cup races.

We trained on the same lake, we had the same coach, some days we even car-pooled to training; it was easy to be teammates and yet, without question, we were competitors. The first race of our series was a World Cup in Duisburg, Germany. Just as we were about to go, Silken was injured, so she couldn't make the trip. Our first head-to-head would have to wait, but I won the race and was able to collect some significant World Cup points.

I flew back to Victoria to race in the Canadian small-boat championship, but Silken was still not ready to compete and withdrew. Our best-of-five series was disintegrating. After a fairly easy win in Victoria, I flew to Paris and then Henley, England, for the second and third World Cup races. My fifth-place result in Paris was disappointing, but the win at the Henley regatta solidified my position as the 1994 World Cup champion. With one race left, it was almost impossible for anyone to take the crystal World Cup trophy from me. But I still had something to prove; I needed to race against Silken.

The final women's single World Cup race of the season took place in Lucerne, Switzerland. I agreed to let it be a winner-takes-all race between Silken and me to determine who would represent Canada at the Worlds. She was the Olympic bronze medallist in this event, and on top of my current sculling success, I was a world and Olympic champion from sweep rowing. The rowing world eagerly awaited our showdown almost as much as I did.

I wanted this victory for more than just the right to race at the World Championships. It was as if Silken were my big sister and I had felt a bit overshadowed by her. Although we'd been on the same team for five years, I wasn't sure she had ever respected the accomplishments of my sweep teammates and me. If I could beat her in this race, maybe she'd give us the credit I believed we deserved.

It was a race of the titans. Silken always had incredible power, and the start of this race was no exception. She jumped to a lead, and I had to trust my race plan, which was to catch up and pass her as we rowed through the middle section of the race. I was able to catch up, but I struggled, and eventually failed to pass. It was a hard race, both physically and emotionally. Racing in the single was still unusually quiet for me; Kathleen wasn't there to inspire me. I had no one to talk to, no one to work with. It was a great race, and to this day it still torments me. I remember most of my negative dialogue and very few bits of my positive.

But for all of the negatives that I remember, it was the fastest race that women had ever rowed. Silken and I both had the race of our lives; neither of us would ever row a faster race again. Silken had set a new world's-best time, and even my time of 7 minutes, 20 seconds crushed the previous course record. My first thought when I crossed the finish line was pride that I'd given everything. My second thought was "Damn!" because I had lost and I really wanted to beat her. How about that for embracing duality! It had been a phenomenally fast race, but I was second. I was definitely a jammed cat! My next thoughts went back to every stroke I had taken in the race to see if there was something that I could have done better to go just a little bit faster, and of course there were more than a few moments in the race that I second-guessed.

Away from the moment, it was easy to poke holes in my technique and even my resolve during the race. It's crazy for me to realize that as I got closer to my perfect race, I also got closer to quitting. To go as hard and fast as you possibly can means that you are on the brink of collapse; it is a fine balance. Too controlled and I'll go too slow; too aggressive is inefficient and I won't have enough energy to make it to the finish.

Today, I have to make an effort to remember that I crossed that finish line and, even though I didn't win, I was really proud of my race. I'd done everything "right," but I also always remember a bit of panic; I was almost off balance. In hindsight I recall thinking of quitting during that race. If I hadn't thought that, could I have gone faster? Was I weak? No—to go that fast I couldn't have been. But my mind won't let go of the idea that I was.

Being ambitious for more is what forces us to remember those moments that we'd like to improve. The flash thought to quit mid-race—why do I always remember that? It was my fastest race; I won the World Cup (overall) trophy that day. Satisfied yet unsatisfied; it wasn't quite perfect. It reminds me how much I don't want to quit—anything—because the memory of quitting lingers. But it also reminds me of the amazing speed I was capable of when I was almost off balance.

For highly ambitious people, there is always something left to tweak. I think we intentionally remember what we are unsatisfied with more than what we are satisfied with, so that we know where to improve. If we have a desire to achieve more, we will use all of our experiences to keep us accountable to our goal. We need to try for perfect, but we have to let go of the idea of *being* perfect.

STARK RAVING BONKERS:
YOU'VE GOT MORE THAN YOU KNOW

It's one thing to accept, while you are training and preparing, that you don't know your limits; but it's quite another to accept, during your big challenge, that you really are capable of doing more.

The Canadian rowing team went to Essen, Germany, in May 1992 to race in a European Cup regatta. Al Morrow, our coach, knew that the format of these regattas is compressed to maximize the number of race opportunities in one weekend. That was perfect for the Canadian team, because we wanted to get as much racing experience as possible. Even though it wasn't the international norm, each Canadian rower had been preparing to race in two events, either the pair and the eight or the four and the eight. What Al didn't know when he entered us was how the European teams adjusted their entries to match the regatta format. While the German or Romanian rowers might enter two events at World Cup regattas, here they were sure to enter only one each day. They were racing only their small boats (the pair and four) on the Saturday and only their eight on the Sunday.

A World Championship regatta takes a week. Over seven days a rower could have up to four races: the heat, repechage (a last-chance race before elimination), semifinal, and final for one event. It was extraordinarily rare for a rower to race twice in one day. Anything less than twenty-four hours to recover between races was considered extremely demanding. Racing two events there is very rarely done. At a World Cup regatta the four stages are compressed into three days and sometimes only two. This European Cup regatta schedule, heats through to finals, was compressed into just *one* day. Then the full schedule was repeated the next day. No one entered two events on the same day. No one, that is, except us.

I raced in the pair and the eight on Saturday and again on Sunday. Because there were over fifteen pairs on Saturday, a semifinal would be necessary to determine the six boats for the final. In the other events, there was no semifinal; the top two from the heats would go directly to the final. (I can't even imagine how the race count would have piled up if we hadn't been in the top two and would have had to go to any of the repechages.)

The best-case scenario for those of us racing in the pair and the eight would be five races on Saturday and another four races on Sunday. The women racing in the four didn't have it much easier; their two-day total of races would be eight. When we pointed this out to Al, he reminded us why we had come to Essen: to get as much race experience as possible. It was an Olympic year, and we needed to become as familiar as possible with our international opponents. We would learn something from every race, Al said. This was going to be one hell of a weekend.

Saturday between 9 AM and 4 PM we raced the pair heat, the eight heat, the pair semi, the pair final, and then the eight final. We adjusted our normal warm-ups and cool-downs, planned appropriate meals and snacks, and focussed on the task of a busy and difficult day. We won every race that day except the fifth and last, our eight final. The Romanians beat us by almost four seconds, which is a lot, even for a European Cup race.

After the eight final, we dragged our tired bodies to a debriefing session for day one. I'm not sure what we expected, but it wasn't to be scolded for letting the Romanians beat us by as much as they did. "Where was the fight?" Al asked. Perhaps we expected some leniency after racing as many as five races, but he was critical of our effort! Our posture was slumped, our timing was off, and we didn't look as crisp as usual, he said. He challenged us to attack the Romanians the next day, suggesting that we had just gone through the motions.

We were pissed off at him. Did he have any idea of what we had just done? Five races in a day was hard! We had half expected a pat on the back from our coach, but instead we received only a demand for more.

The next morning came too quickly. Our bodies wanted more time to rest and recover, but day two was set to begin. We had been very well prepared and had come to the regatta amazingly fit. Even with all of the fatigue from the previous day of racing, the pair and the eight advanced directly to the finals after the heats. I began to really worry that I wouldn't have enough energy left for the last two races. In the back of my mind, I still heard Al's scolding about the eight. It made me angry to think that he would be expecting more from the eight today.

Our biggest competition in the pair final would be the German pair, two-time world champions. We had been their nemesis last year and had beaten them again the day before. This was an Olympic year, and we did not want them to learn that beating us was ever possible. But when it was time for this afternoon race, my body was not recovering as it had in the morning. The race didn't go the way we hoped. Kathleen made a small technical mistake in the first few strokes, and the German crew took advantage of her rare error. They established a comfortable lead that we were not able to erase. At 1,500 metres I made a mistake that cost us the race.

Our race plan was a very detailed program that united and motivated us through a 2,000-metre race course. There were three distinct phases: the start, the body, and the finish. Even with Kathleen's mistake, we had re-attacked the start, getting the boat moving from a dead stop and into the middle 1,000 metres—the body phase—of the race. At the 1,500-metre mark, coming into the finish phase, I should have called Plan A.

Plan A is an all-out sprint, but I called Plan B. It gets used only in situations that require a minimum effort to advance;

it's an energy management tool. We always preferred to win because that would earn us a better lane assignment in the final (the centre lanes are preferred), but that is a nice-to-have; getting into the final is the need-to-have. If we were in a semifinal where the top three boats would advance to the final, then we would need to spend only enough energy to get us into that group. When we could avoid it, we would never go all out (Plan A) in a semifinal. It's helpful to keep an ace in the hole.

When I made the decision to call Plan B, it meant that we would not sprint to the finish. I felt that we were clearly in second place, and with only 500 metres to go I let the little doubting voices of mind and body talk me into choosing less. This was, after all, our eighth international race in two days, but only the fifth for the German crew. How were we going to muster another attack for the eight in less than an hour? I was thinking ahead already; we had another race to row after this. Strategy was my role, and I called Plan B; Kathleen tacitly agreed.

After the race, which we finished in second, Al's steel-blue eyes and flushed face clearly showed that he was furious. It had been obvious that we hadn't attacked. What happened? When I explained "our" choice to accept second and conserve the little energy that we might have left for the eight, he lost it. We had been gaining on the Germans, he said. With a sprint we could have won and maintained the mental advantage going into the rest of the season. Instead we had taught them that we could be beaten.

I didn't think it was fair that Al should be disappointed in us for not going for it. I told Al how our bodies felt. We were tapped out of energy, and I had made a decision based on what

I thought was a strategic choice to have a chance to attack in the eight. He would hear none of it and told us to get ready; it was time to race against the Romanians. All of the Canadians had already raced more races in this one weekend than we had all of last year. The warm-up was quiet but focussed. Our coxie reminded us of Al's instruction to stick more closely to the Romanians than we'd done yesterday.

As we rowed the warm-up for the race, I was angry and terrified. This was my ninth race; how could I possibly manage? None of us were complaining, so I assumed that the rest of my team was fine. How was I going to keep up with them? I felt that my body wouldn't last the whole race, so I made another choice. My coach had accused me of under-pacing and conserving in the pair, so I was going to show him! He was going to have to watch me hit the wall. I was going to attack just as he wanted, and if I didn't make it to the finish line—then so be it!

It went by so quickly. The race started and we attacked. I made a conscious effort to be someone who contributes more. In an eight, with so many people making the boat move, it can be easy to almost hide. If you put your oar in the water with everyone and take it out with everyone, you can get away with not pulling particularly hard. If I wasn't going to make it all the way to the finish line, it wasn't going to be because I was "just along for the ride"; on every stroke I gave my crew everything I had (as, I'm quite sure, all of my teammates were doing too).

As we went down the course, I knew my teammates were as tired as I was. I wasn't going to be the first to lessen my load, so I continued to pull my oar and push the water by. Before I knew it, our coxie, Lesley Thompson, was calling for our sprint to the finish—Plan A. With every stroke that we took, part of me was waiting for my body to max out, but I still felt connected to the work; I was still contributing to our speed. The Romanians were ahead, but not by much at all. When they attacked, we did too. All weekend they had raced only the eight, so with fresher legs they moved ahead by just a bit more.

At the finish line, Romania was first by just over a second. I had never been so surprised by my body. Even with our incredible buildup of fatigue, we had decreased the gap by three seconds. I had so much more to tap into than I had previously believed.

Al was right, which meant that I was wrong, much as I hated to admit it. If I had that much energy to give to the eight, then I had missed an opportunity in the pair. At the very least, we should have tried. I would never fail to try again. Regret, like fear of failure, can be a tremendous motivator if you carry it correctly. I am proud to always carry that regret with me.

When the regatta was over and our boats were loaded on the trailer to go to our next training location, I sat with my teammates under a tree. A British rower came over and asked us if we were the Canadians who had raced nine races in two days. Proud and exhausted, we all nodded. "I just want to say," she said, "I think you are all stark raving bonkers!" I loved it. I thought it would make a great line on a T-shirt: "Stark Raving Bonkers."

Sometimes I wonder if Al made a mistake when he entered us in all of those races. Physiologically it was insane. Psychologically it turned out to be a master stroke. Racing two events at the world or Olympic level is considered risky because of the lack of recovery and the accumulation of fatigue. We had every intention of racing two events each at the Olympics. In Essen, we learned that we could survive nine races in two days.

When we got to the Olympics, the worst-case scenario meant that we would race seven times in seven days; the best case would be five races in seven days. Seven whole days for only five races! We had never raced with that amount of recovery time.

Canada won the pair, the four, and the eight at the 1992 Olympics. In the eight, the Romanians didn't know what had hit them. At the Olympics, with over twenty-four hours of recovery time after racing our small boats, not only did we beat them, we beat them by almost four seconds—which is huge for an Olympic final.

EGO IS NOT THE SAME AS ARROGANCE

Ego, I believe, is an essential trait in the pursuit of more. It means that you believe in yourself and your abilities, that you feel you are able. Your ego doesn't tell you that you *will* do something, but it tells you that you *can* do something. Ego is respectful to those around you—competitors, teammates, and people who have similar goals. The words *ego* and *arrogance* are often mistakenly used interchangeably; but ego and arrogance are very different.

Having an ego, being ready, and feeling confident are like having a secret. Your competition can only wonder what it is that you know that others don't. Ego can be intimidating. When confident people enter a room, a boathouse, or an office, they seem to almost swagger. The sense of readiness and pre-paredness radiates from them.

Too much arrogance doesn't present the same threat at all; it actually suggests insecurity. When performers have to work hard to convince those around them that they are good or that they should win, then it is not so hard to think that they haven't quite convinced themselves. Although the subtle and genuine presentation of a healthy ego seems to leave competitors only *hoping* to win, boastful arrogance doesn't sell itself as well.

Is it possible to have an ego and no arrogance? Probably not completely; the line can be fine. Different people draw the line in different places. My ego tended to be obvious, but I'd like to think that I kept my arrogance in check. Even Kathleen, who had a remarkably low level of arrogance for the ego that she had, was accused of being arrogant—once. She told a German reporter before a race that we would win that race and go on to win at the Olympic Games later in the year. It was meant simply as a confident statement but was received by the German audience as astoundingly arrogant. (This sort of statement was so unusual from Kathleen that many people attributed it, and its arrogance, to me! I may have thought it too, but I never said it—at least not to the German press.)

Arrogance may come from fear and uncertainty. In an effort to convince themselves that they are ready and confident, arrogant people get caught trying too hard to convince others. The bravado that comes from arrogance shows a lack of respect not only for others but also for the task and goal that are being attempted.

There is little less appealing than arrogance: boasting, bragging, and—possibly the worst characteristic of an arrogant person—feeling entitled, as if success is his or her due, simply *because.*

BE BETTER, NOT BITTER

During my university rowing career, our University of Western Ontario crew would travel each spring to Philadelphia for the Dad Vail Regatta. It was a "shirts" regatta, which meant that there was a friendly wager of our racing singlets. With thirty boats in the women's varsity eight race, if you won, each member of the winning crew would go home with an extra twenty-nine slightly used and sweaty tops.

Like most Canadian university rowing teams, and unlike some of the U.S. college teams we were about to race against, we were on a shoestring budget. When the crew from the United States Naval Academy showed up, they looked very professional. They had a new boat and new blades and wore a new uniform that included more than just the singlet and rowing jacket that we had. They had a beautiful tent that their supporters put up, and a handsome new truck pulled their boat trailer. The Navy rowers walked around the boat storage area dripping with arrogance. No one looked as good as they did, and I guess we were to infer that they were supposed to win.

We may not have been as well funded, but we were well trained and ready to race. I saw their new bright yellow and blue singlets and new boat but didn't see anything from them on the water that we couldn't beat with a good race. And that's what we did. Western won the Dad Vail Regatta, and after the race, as we were putting our boat onto the trailer to go home, twenty-eight college crews came over, congratulated us, and gave us their race singlets. Everyone we raced against came over except Navy. They were very bitter about the loss. The win was supposed to be theirs.

The next year we went back to Dad Vail. Once again Navy arrived with another fancy new boat, new oars, and bright yellow and blue uniforms. We had the same equipment as before, and some of us may have had the same singlet. And again we came well prepared and ready to race. We noticed that Navy had added a piece to their uniform—a baseball cap with their N on the front and a single word on the back: "Bitter."

Their arrogance had kept them bitter for a whole year! Did they really think that we had taken something from them that they were entitled to? Their arrogance made me want to beat them that much more. And we did. I thought it would be fun to get a baseball cap too; our word on the back would be "Better." I never went home with a Navy singlet, but that's okay, because Western went home with the win.

I'd rather be better than bitter any day. Ego is way more powerful and productive when it's real, and that's not arrogance.

Sometimes a tremendous amount of ego can appear to be arrogance, but even the most humble of athletes need to have ego to be successful. You can't win if you don't believe you are ready. At times, the Canadian Olympic kayaker and gold, silver, and bronze medallist Adam van Koeverden tends to appear very arrogant. But knowing Adam, I believe he is just so extremely confident that his training, in its volume and intensity, matches or betters that of any of his competitors that when he talks honestly about it, he sounds boastful.

The British rower Matthew Pinsent was so confident in the preparation that he and his partner had done for an upcoming race that he was convinced that there was no crew in the world that could possibly beat them. What I saw him do definitely bordered on arrogance but was possibly the biggest display of confidence and ego I've ever seen. Right before the 1994 World Cup race in Lucerne, Matt came very close to wishing his opponent all the best for winning silver. He meant to be encouraging, saying "hope you beat the Germans too," but it came over as good luck getting the silver because we will have the gold. He had no idea how arrogant he sounded to his opponent and, when I pointed it out to him, he regretted his choice of words. But as Matt said, his "arrogance leaked out a bit that day." Matt's no-option-but-first confidence was fuelled by a belief in the training that he and his partner,

Steve Redgrave, had undergone. He believed in it and wasn't afraid to use it as a tool to keep himself pushing for more. For him, the goal was deeply set in stone. I noted and admired his determination to win and, as much as I would try to externalize it more gently, I knew that it was part of his secret for success.

Matt and Steve had the track record to support their self-confidence, but ego can show itself differently, even within the same team. For three years they had been world and Olympic champions, dominating the men's pair event. Steve was universally respected, not only for his success as a rower but also because of the type of competitor he was. There was simply an air to Steve that made him appear to always be ready; you could see that he was confident, but I never heard it from him. Arguably he had more reason to have a big ego than Matt, but Steve's always seemed internalized. They shared their complete faith in their preparations. Both had ego, but only one actively revealed it.

In the end, Matt and Steve did win the race, and they set a world record in the process. Their ego had been well founded, but Matt had not earned much respect from his competitors with his über-confident comment. As Matt matured and became comfortable with his successes, he internalized some of his ego. After an incredibly successful career, he is respected not just for being a great racer but also for being a genuine champion. A big element in becoming a career champion is to be aware of how you externalize your ego and to whom. You should still plan to win; you just don't need to announce it!

I've been told by some of the women we raced against that when Kathleen and I got to a regatta, we looked as if we owned the place. We didn't seem to care what anyone else was doing. (If I were to admit it, I was likely more like Matt, and Kathleen was more private, like Steve.) While we respectfully acknowledged our competitors, our ego showed itself as an air of confidence. That was actually pretty far from the truth, but it was nice to know that others saw us that way.

I admit that without Kathleen, I probably would have seemed more arrogant than I would have liked. It wasn't uncommon for me to be a bit brash, and Kathleen was extremely uncomfortable with that. As a result, when we were together I would try to contain myself. Thanks to her, I believe I learned to be more respectful.

Can ego be over-controlled? I think so. Ego has inertia. The law of inertia states that a body in motion stays in motion and a body at rest stays at rest. In sport, that could be translated as success breeding more success, which feeds confidence. Efforts to control and internalize your natural ego may do harm to your momentum and performance. You can try too hard to look humble. If you detach yourself from your past successes or future potential, you risk detaching from your ego, and your confidence can drop. If you prefer to be quiet, that's fine; internalize your ego—but don't detach from it.

Hopefully, doing what feels right to you will also be respectful to others around you. Different sports and corporate environments have vastly varying cultures and accepted behaviour, so you should be careful about emulating what you see on TV or from afar. In trying not to appear arrogant, or trying to look as if you have more ego than you do, you can sometimes stifle your own confidence. You have to be your own person.

REDIRECT

Sometimes you must adjust your goal or embrace a new one on the fly. This does not mean that you were not committed and accountable to your goal. Nor does it mean that you failed or that you quit. Putting your goal in stone indicated that you wanted to give it a real try. But not every goal-achieving path goes as planned. Sometimes a new passion can evolve or legitimate reasons can pile up that force you to reassess the path you are on. You may have to rethink the whole goal or just the little things that you do every day. In either case, you need to be flexible.

As a result of following your goal-achieving path, you may stumble on something unexpected that piques your curiosity and sends you in a completely new direction. Consider an athlete with a passion for sport who, as a hobby, takes photos of his journey. One day he discovers that his skills and passion for photography outweigh those for his sport; he is good at doing his sport, but he finds he is great at capturing it. His ambition can shift entirely, and that is a good thing; it's part of the process. It's not that he gave up on the idea of going to the Olympics; he just found his next step—and maybe a different way of getting to the Games.

Goal setting is not always linear; where you want to go doesn't always reflect where you are or where you have been. Sometimes the right goal for you can look like a step backwards to everyone else. After ten years of being first or second in the world, I would never have expected to celebrate being last in a race. But I would have missed out on a fabulous opportunity if I hadn't.

As I explained earlier, there are cycles within each year, and some times—some days, some weeks, some seasons—felt harder than others. Careers are like that too; not every year will be a banner year. It is easy to take responsibility when a plan is working and you improve or win, but when things go poorly, it's just as important that you own that moment too. The market, the competition, and your health will constantly vary, and your goal setting has to take this into account. Sometimes you have to acknowledge that you aren't progressing along your goal-achieving path as planned. If you don't, you won't be able to make any of the necessary adjustments to succeed in the future. There is no point in banging your head against the same brick wall over and over again.

Toward the middle of the 1998 race season, for the second time in my career, I found myself racing the single. I had been the 1993 silver medallist and the 1994 overall World Cup champion in the single, but I returned to racing the double with Kathleen Heddle. My training and racing experience showed. In late 1998, on my own once again, I won the 9-kilometre Armada Cup in Bern, Switzerland, as well as a 420-metre sprint regatta near Brisbane, Australia, re-establishing myself as one of the fastest scullers in the world. I was a legitimate contender for a medal at the 1999 World Championships and had excellent potential for the 2000 Sydney Olympics.

I especially wanted to win a medal at the 1999 Worlds since they were to be held very close to my home, in St. Catharines, Ontario. I had won a dozen world and Olympic medals but never in front of a home crowd. The media were quick to present me as a favourite. They knew that I'd been in this position before, that I had the potential to win, and that I had the experience and talent to turn that potential into success. My goal and my path to achieve it were clearly set.

And then something happened. I don't know what I did, but even though all of my training went well, I started having bad races and then really bad races. There was nothing obviously wrong, but I had a sense for the first time that my body was letting me down. I'd never had many injuries, and although I didn't feel injured, I wasn't recovering the way I used to. At thirty-one, I assumed I was just getting old.

Early that summer I had some success, which kept my hopes up. At the first World Cup race that year I won the bronze medal but, uncharacteristically, I was quite far off the lead. In my next race, I was fifth and an embarrassing fourteen seconds off the lead. This season was not going according to plan.

The Canadian media hounded me for answers—heck, *I* wanted answers. As the season progressed, I was going more and more slowly, regardless of how hard I worked. I sucked it up and simply said that I was struggling and didn't know why. I would have to return to Canada, keep training, and hope that I could find the missing key that would again unlock my speed. My ambition to race well, particularly in front of a home audience, kept me extremely committed. I could have created plenty of excuses—poor health, distracted training, sharing a coach—but I knew that I had no real reason to give the media, or myself.

It was in my nature to stay accountable to my ambitions, but at the same time I needed to make some responsible decisions. I had to accept that I was no longer a favourite to win a medal at the Worlds. I had to adjust my goal for that year from being in the top two to finishing in the top six. For the last ten years I had never placed lower than second. I had to come to terms with the fact that just making the final of the World Championships would be a success. This was not easy to accept.

I couldn't even lower my goals privately. The media were still predicting big things from me. I had to explain to them that I was in a precarious position. I didn't have the speed to make things go easily and according to plan. If the seeding (the initial placement of the rowers into their heats) was unbalanced at all, then come the two semifinal races, there could be an unfair depth of talent in one race compared with the other. The top three would advance from each semi, and a difficult semifinal could easily push me out of the final. I had never failed to make a World Championship final, and the media knew it too.

When the event finally started, I was still struggling to understand what was slowing me down. All I knew was that I still hadn't been able to find my top gear. It would take me another year to discover that I had two bulging discs in my lower back.

Racing began, and for the first time in my career I was not leading my races at the World Championships. But I was still chasing that year's goal, even if it had been redirected mid-season. At the semifinals, there was no thought that I could go with anything but Plan A; it took everything I had to beat the similarly ranked Australian in order to finish third and advance to the final. The Canadian newspapers the next day wrote about my result as if it were a great victory. My rowing friends from around the world were astonished. They all felt that if an Australian, British, or American champion with a career record like mine had barely squeaked into a final, they would have been roasted. Because I hadn't painted a big rosy image to the media and had told them—and more importantly myself—of my situation, they understood my new goal. It turned out that because I owned up to my realistic need to redirect my goal, they became my cheerleaders instead of my critics.

I had really looked at my season and my results and had adjusted my goal to be more realistic. In being as honest about my poor results as I had been about my great results, I was able to adjust my goal setting so that my target, while still very challenging, was achievable. I finished sixth at those World Championships, which for most rowers is a tough thing to swallow. Sixth means you were last in the race. For someone who is normally on the podium, it was even harder. But my redirected goal was top six, and it turned out that to a home crowd who knew what I was racing for, sixth was okay.

EXPECT THE UNEXPECTED

Rarely does everything go as planned. Before every Olympics, part of the advice I give to the team as they prepare is to expect something to happen that could threaten all of their plans. This advice comes from experience.

On the morning of July 27, 1996, I woke up in Atlanta to find a note with an unexpected message slid under our door. It was a big day—really big. Everything that Kathleen and I had done for years had been in preparation for that day; it was the Olympic final for the women's double. I think I had known that the race was going to be at 11 AM for two years. McBean and Heddle were the Olympic favourites.

It wasn't unusual to get a note from Al on the morning of a race. As our coach, he would usually remind us what shuttle bus he was going to take to the rowing course and what time we would all meet. This note was different. We thought we were prepared for anything, but this news caught me completely off guard. "A bomb went off last night in the Centennial Olympic Park. People were injured and possibly killed. Expect security delays and/or cancellations. You may want to get an earlier bus." That was a lot of information, but we were left with more questions than answers.

The Centennial Olympic Park had been designated by Olympic organizers to be a central gathering place for the public. It covered a large city block in downtown Atlanta and was the focal point for open-air concerts, sponsors' hospitality tents, pin exchanges, and Olympic art displays. During the Games tens of thousands of people gathered all day and into the night to celebrate the Olympics.

A bomb? About twenty members of my family had come to Atlanta to watch our races, and I wouldn't have been surprised if they had gone downtown to enjoy the festival atmosphere of an Olympic city. Kathleen had a few family members who had also come to Atlanta to watch. Were our families okay? Cellphones were rare (and the size of a running shoe) then; there was no way to know.

It had been about 5:30 AM when we woke and found the note. Our plan had been to get a 7:00 bus, but now we had to rush to get the 6:30 bus. And was this a terrorist attack? That was the big question as we got ourselves ready to go to breakfast.

Packing to go to an Olympic final requires that you include the podium uniform with a post-race change of clothes. This always seems so presumptuous—putting in your celebration clothes before you have something to celebrate. I've heard of some people who won't pack it, because they are superstitious. I'm pretty sure that no one has ever lost because they were brave enough to pack their podium uniform, but I wouldn't be surprised if there are people who didn't win because they lacked the confidence to pack it. Although Kathleen and I didn't know for sure that we would be on the podium, we were sure that we *could* be. We had to pack for a "normal" day but already this was anything but.

Al always made sure we got thorough briefings before each regatta so we'd know what to expect, but on this morning, arguably the biggest morning of our career, we felt completely uninformed. It was only 6 AM when we went to the cafeteria, so very few people were up; there were no credible updates. Could the Olympics be cancelled? There had been a terrorist attack on athletes at the Munich Olympics in 1972; was this something similar? Were we in danger? This was all happening before the time of twenty-four-hour news stations. Nobody in the village really knew anything.

It's not hard to rush through breakfast on the morning of an Olympic final. We were nervous and could barely eat. We made it to the 6:30 bus, thinking that we would have an advantage over our competition. But all of the others got there shortly after us. Kathleen and I were grateful that we found seats for the fifty-minute ride. The "VIP" transportation for Olympic athletes on their way to an Olympic final was a regular city bus. Sitting on the hard seats, we all found ourselves facing the centre aisle with nothing to look at but each other.

Beyond my worries for my family, my head was reeling with all of the unexpected derailers. How do we handle a delay? Did I put enough food in my bag to manage that? What about a really long delay? Kathleen and I were entered in two races, and our second final was at 10:40 AM the next day. We wanted as much time as possible between races for our bodies to recover. To win the quad race would require a fresh effort. What about cancellations? I hardly believed that events would be cancelled, but I had to anticipate that possibility. That's what we'd been taught to do. Kathleen and I were doing everything we could. We had built in extra time to deal with security delays, and now all we could do was wait.

I get sick if I read in buses or cars, so for fifty minutes I had nothing to do but listen to music and think. I looked at our competitors and saw how focussed and anxious they looked. Quite likely, I looked the same to them, but that's not entirely how I was feeling.

I started to think that I *should* be anxious and worried. Even with everything going on, I realized how relaxed I actually was. Sitting beside Kathleen, I was completely confident in everything that we had done to get us to that point. We had developed a language between us where single words referred to paragraphs of information. For all of our differences, all it took was a look or a nod to know that we were strong together. We had always figured out how to work through injury, conflict, and our fair share of drama. We had been taught to anticipate change and challenge.

It didn't matter if things were going to keep going crazy all day. Our cup was full with our preparation. We were ready for anything. It felt great knowing that.

When we finally got to Lake Lanier, the Olympic rowing venue, the security forces with their dogs did a full search of the bus's undercarriage and exterior. We were grateful to be on an earlier bus than normal because they were making an extra effort, and it took forever.

As the bus sat there, we opened the windows to let in some cool, fresh air and could hear the sounds of the grandstand. An announcement came over the PA system asking everyone to stand and observe a moment of silence for the people who had been killed and injured the night before. This meant that the pre-race protocol had begun. The races were a go. It was a sober moment in the stands but in the bus, I have to admit, everyone breathed a little easier. It was game on!

Finally, we got off the bus and met Al. He was able to give us some real information about what had happened the night before and the status of racing that day. A large pipe bomb had gone off after 1 AM near a bench close to a concert. Over a hundred people had been injured, and at least one person had been killed. The FBI very quickly announced that they believed the bombing to be the work of a lone-wolf perpetrator and not an organized attack.

That put an end to the guessing and speculation. Once we heard the time of the blast and the band's name, we relaxed. Jack Mack and the Heart Attack was not the type of band that would have attracted our families. I felt confident that they were all in the stands, decked out in red and white, ready to cheer us on. Games on!

The bomb had the potential to derail us. We could have stressed out and panicked simply from a lack of information. It was a close race, and a little bit of lost energy could have changed the outcome. Instead we trusted that we were ready for anything.

Something unexpected happens along almost every goal-achieving path. Rarely will it be as dramatic as a bomb threatening the entire Olympic schedule, but unplanned and unfortunate things will happen. When we are confident in our preparation and communication, the likelihood that a team can push for more is high. In case of emergency—check your (preparation) cup.

BREATHE AND OUTLAST

I have only one superstition, really. When it comes to getting into the start gates, it's "Never first, never last."

Kathleen and I liked to move into our lane as soon as the race before ours had gone past. We wanted to get a few warm-up strokes in at the pace we would race at. Each boat must be in its lane and in the start position between three and five minutes ahead of the start. If you get too far out, you have to scramble to get back. You want to be warmed up in the start but not out of breath.

Each of the six lanes has a dock at one end with a ramp sticking out from it like a diving board. We back our boat into position, where a young volunteer lying on the ramp will simply hold onto the end of it until the start signal. I liked to get into my preferred place ("Never the first boat to be ready, never last") for no reason other than that it gives me something to think about. Once you're in, all that is left to do is race.

In Atlanta, as always, it seemed so quiet in the start gates, with just a few whispered final words between the rowers. The only other sound was from the photographers and the official aligning the boats. When I looked over my shoulder to check that we were straight in the lane, our 2,000-metre course looked like 200,000 metres.

I'm known for always talking. I talk everywhere, except at the start of a race. Here there was nothing to say. I knew we were ready to go. Sitting still and just waiting was the worst part. We had to sit still for less than five minutes, but it felt like forever. It seemed as if I could feel my heart beating in my arms; my heart rate was revved and ready to go.

I used to struggle for something meaningful to say to Kathleen at these times. How could I have words for every occasion and then, on this one, come up empty? In trying to figure out what to say to Kathleen, I usually wondered what I needed to say to myself. After many big, stressful races, it boiled down to two words. That's all we would need here: *breathe* and *outlast*.

Breathe. The first time I said "Breathe" to Kathleen in the start gates, it was because I was so nervous I was forgetting to breathe myself; I needed some air. As soon as I said it, I saw

Kathleen take the same big inhalation that I did—and then we released it. It calmed both of us down; we simply focussed on the task at hand.

With very little time left until the start command would be given to us, I'd say the only word left that would mean anything: "Outlast." I'd watch Kathleen's head nod; she knew what it meant, and she agreed.

Itching to go, there was nothing left to do but wait for the starter's command. Finally, "Attention..." After a pause that seemed like minutes instead of seconds, an electronic beep released us.

Kathleen and I had a very detailed race plan. We followed it through a series of technical and power focus phases. After seven years of racing, we had perfected a thirty-stroke power burst through the halfway mark. Everyone knew to expect this bit from us, so for this Olympic final we added a few attack bursts just before and after. Where traditionally we had been steady, we now wanted to catch the others off guard.

Four years earlier, in the Barcelona Olympic final, in the middle of the race I had allowed myself a moment of confidence that the race was ours. It was a naive lapse of focus that could have led to any number of technical mistakes. I was smarter by 1996. Now experience wouldn't allow my mind to wander; I was far too aware of the mistakes that can result. The first half of the race was well executed; we were focussed and together. We had a bit of a lead, but not much.

As always, the burst through the middle shot us clear into the lead. We were rowing very well, but still, I had a sense that the energy cost of those extra bursts had been high. We were coming into the last 500 metres and I wasn't sure how I was going to be able to hold on. The Chinese, the Dutch, and the Germans all began aggressive moves to catch us. That final 500 metres would take us another one minute and forty-five seconds, and I was already struggling.

This is where we really needed to remember that rallying cry: "Outlast." The countless workouts that we had done with and against each other as well as the rest of our Canadian team had taught us that there was no such thing as a hard workout that is hard on only one person. We knew that everyone in this race would be hurting as much as we were. So when the pain and the doubts started to crash over us in waves, there was only one thing left to do: outlast them all.

With 250 metres left to go in the race, we saw the red lane buoys, signifying that we were nearing the finish. Eighteen thousand spectators were going crazy; the noise was deafening. I had to shout the last few bits of our race plan so that Kathleen could hear me. This was not the place to mistime an attack. The Chinese and the Dutch were getting very close. They felt way too close.

With ten strokes left, we still had the lead. There was no reason left to watch the other boats—they were still coming as hard as they could, so we just had to go as hard as we could too. The problem was that I was done. I felt completely spent.

I will never be sure that, if I had been by myself, I wouldn't have just curled up in a ball and let the other boats go through. But that wasn't an option in this partnership. There wasn't a chance I was going to quit on Kathleen. I took my motivation from the fact that she still kept taking the next stroke, so I kept taking that next stroke with her. There wasn't a chance I'd let her feel that she was carrying the whole load either. If I was taking a stroke with her, I was giving 100 per cent of what I had to that stroke.

I didn't think I had ten strokes in me—actually, I was pretty sure I didn't—but I took one more with Kathleen. It was all I needed to do—I could take one more stroke with Kathleen. I was just as certain I didn't have the remaining nine, but I took each one of those too.

And it happened. I took each one more stroke with Kathleen until the next one more was the final one. It was just a stroke, no bigger or stronger than any other stroke we had taken, but it put us across the finish line. It was probably a pretty ugly stroke if you consider the fatigue and stress that were layered into it, but it was all we had. We gave it 100 per cent of everything we had left.

Olympic champions. *Breathe.*

I have many less intense tasks now where I still use this "just one more" mantra to get me through. Bike rides, runs, even some large spreadsheets that I need to fill out for work can be daunting. Whether I am struggling with a massive task or a mundane one, if I don't think I can finish the whole thing, I don't force my mind to wrap itself around that. I break it down into manageable bits; take it one stride, one column, one bit more at a time. "Infinity plus one"—$\infty+1$—is how I've said I define my personal philosophy. Remember, you don't need to be a superhero. You reach for infinity by adding as many "one mores" as you can.

7

SUCCESS
and CONFIDENCE

YOU would think that being an Olympic champion is all glory and celebration. All of the work and the stress and even the finish line are behind you; and the title Olympic champion is for life! It puts a little extra swagger in your step; perhaps you even let yourself feel a bit like a superhero. Your life, you would think, would be pretty charmed from there. For about forty minutes in Atlanta, that's what I thought.

Crossing an Olympic finish line first is amazing. So many of the moments that followed in 1996 were exactly what I had always dreamt of. Mixed with the stunning pain that coursed through my muscles and the hot, heaving contractions of my lungs were the thoughts, first, "Thank God I didn't screw up" and then "YES! We did it!"

In front of my family and friends, in front of thousands of spectators, and with a television audience that I can't begin to estimate, we had achieved Olympic supremacy. In all of the mental imagery I had done, conjuring up the hardest and most gruelling races, I could not have imagined the enormous swelling of pride I felt now; I must have been beaming. Even with the physical pain of the race, I felt an incredible euphoria.

The mental toll of racing at the Olympics does not get easier with experience; returning medallists actually have more to think about, not less. After winning our third Olympic gold medal, we were exhausted as never before. As always, the first thing we did after the race was thank and congratulate each other. Sitting in the boat, still heaving from the effort of the seven-minute race (and the seven-year effort), Kathleen and I moved in the boat so that I could give her a hug. She lay back toward me and I reached forward; we got stuck there. So exhausted, she didn't have one more sit-up, and I could barely push at all. It took some time for Kathleen and me to row over to the media dock.

We were utterly and completely spent, but we were on top of the world. In our post-race interview, the reporter went on about the fact that we were the first Canadians to ever win three Olympic gold medals. The rowing community was awed by our ability to win in both sweep (the pair in 1992) and now sculling (the double). After the interviews, we rowed over to the medal presentation dock. My heart and ego were soaring at this point. On all of the crappy, cold, and miserable days when I had wanted to give up, this was what had kept me on my path. I was so proud that we had actually done it. This success was awesome. I felt awesome!

Trumpets played a fanfare. An announcer introduced the official procession, and we marched to the podium with the

Chinese and Dutch rowers. Even though my body was still threatening to collapse from our race effort, in my heart I was riding high. An Olympic gold medal was placed around my neck and a bouquet of flowers put in my arms. Kathleen and I exchanged a look that spoke of all the highs and lows of our career—we'd done it. Then the wave: that iconic Olympic wave with the medals glittering, arms stretched high, the bouquets in one hand. It is a champion's moment, and I enjoyed every little bit of it.

Having an Olympic gold medal around your neck, with your national anthem being played, is a fantasy. Some people who don't even do sports have had this as a dream. It had been my goal, and now this was my moment—for a third time, no less. I was in some shock.

Physically, I was struggling, but I still tried to just enjoy what a fantastic moment it was. I tried to still my mind and be present; I watched the flag and sang our anthem. (We did make sure that the music and our words to "O Canada" matched up this time. Thankfully the Americans, unlike the Spanish, played the song in its entirety.)

But in the pursuit of more, feeling both satisfied and unsatisfied, it is hard to switch off quickly. The dialogue in my head fixated for a bit on the fact that there was no wind to flutter the flags. My mental picture of this moment, the one that connected back via thousands of other images to a young girl learning to row, showed the whole flag with its beautiful colours and maple leaf. Of course it wasn't too tough to let that "disappointment" go and enjoy the anthem. We had waved to eighteen thousand spectators. We had been successful; I felt like a champion through and through. My ego was bursting!

It didn't take long after stepping off the podium for my ego to be brought right back down. Once again it was a "task" that reminded me what was really important. We had to row back to the dock by the boat sheds, where Al was waiting with a very proud smile. He shook our hands and gave us each a quick hug. He wasn't alone; we had been selected for a post-race drug test, which was no surprise; all of the medallists would be tested. It's part of the process. After every performance, even an Olympic final, win or lose, life moves on.

The drug test would require us to provide the attending physician with a urine sample. We were directed to a trailer that was set up like a small medical office. In non-sport environments, people provide their own doctors with urine samples all of the time. The process is a little different for athletes. Just as in their competitions, athletes have to perform in an exposed setting. The door to the toilet must remain open, and the athlete must pull her top up to her bra straps, and her pants must go down below her knees. This is to ensure that the urine sample provided can be witnessed and that it does, in fact, come directly from the athlete. This procedure does not make one feel like a hero!

It gets more humbling. Men have it easy. They can see the cup, and their aim is far more under their control. But there I was, forty-five minutes after winning a historic third gold medal, my ego exploding with the idea that I have become someone special. And I am squatting over a toilet with my Olympic racing uniform at my knees and a T-shirt tucked up into my bra. A nurse was trying not to stare, but she was watching as I peed not only into the cup but also on my hand. Awesome—so not a hero.

We had done something great, but that moment always reminds me to keep my feet on the ground. Success may provide you with things, but it does not make you into something more; it does not change you. If you were an ass before you won, you will be an ass after. If you were a normal person, you will still be a normal person.

Achieving some success should add to your confidence to create new goals and start on new journeys. It should fuel an intense belief in your ability to prepare, to remain accountable through many challenges, and to stay committed. Success means that you have been doing things right. Celebrate your victories; then wash your hands and move on.

YOUR NEXT DOOR

I've often said that learning something is like opening a door that leads to a corridor of ten doors. (Why ten? It's just a nice doable number. Maybe your corridors have four doors, maybe twelve. It doesn't matter—because as you'll learn, there are always more doors!) The doors are all labelled. In the beginning the words on the labels are for broad topics such as sport, art, business, science, or family. It's our curiosity that encourages us to reach for a doorknob. We might *think* that once we've opened the ten doors, we will *know* that topic. The truth, however, is that each door leads to another corridor of ten doors. Ambition to learn, curiosity, the pursuit of more can be limitless—if you let it be.

Years ago, after opening a few doors, I reached for the sport door and went down that corridor. I checked out a few of the doors and explored some of their corridors—baseball, soccer, basketball, skiing—but my curiosity about them took me only so far. I kept trying other doors and corridors because the learning was fun.

When I found the rowing door, I was more than intrigued. I went flying in, opening every door that I could reach. Each door I opened led to another ten doors. I had a voracious appetite for learning about rowing; I wanted to know more. This learning was more than just fun; it became my passion. As we learn something, we begin to realize that there is so much more that we want to learn. The broad topics were replaced with increasingly specific ones as I progressed from one learning corridor to the next. Delving into as many corridors and their doors as possible is what made Kathleen and me champions.

Learning something new is exciting because when the doors lead to broad topics, we learn a tremendous amount quickly. Every day can bring a significant positive change. As learning becomes technical, it also becomes subtle. As learning becomes harder because it is more specific, the effect on our performance is less obvious.

Learning something new can also be intimidating. If you have been following one path for a long time, it's not likely that you have dramatically changed directions recently. Learning can also bring a daunting change of pace. The shift from a specific methodical focus on one task to the broad strokes and endless possibilities of new concepts can be dramatic. Change and challenge: anticipate it. Embrace it.

At some point we have to try a new direction altogether. Most of the doors I open aren't rowing doors anymore. As an Olympic mentor, I'm using what I know from rowing and applying that as I learn about other sports and their cultures. But my curiosity takes me everywhere; how does my garden grow, how does my city work? I want to know more about writing and publishing, speaking, broadcasting, adventure, relationships. There is so much to learn, and so much of what we learn from one thing can be applied to so many others.

I'm in no rush to become a one-trick pony again, but it might happen. As I explore the many options that my curiosity presents to me, I just may find the next big goal that I want to apply most—or all—of my ambition to. Until then, I'm quite happy to spread it out among many goals.

We can never stop learning. Being inquisitive might be the most consistent trait among the career champions that I know. Allowing themselves to pursue their curiosity, wherever it may have taken them, is how they discovered what they wanted to do, where they wanted to go, or where they wanted to try next. Learning never ends. Knowledge is power. You will never know what's next unless you open a few doors.

PERSPECTIVE

We often lack perspective on what we are doing because we are too busy doing it. I've climbed Mount Kilimanjaro twice, and after both times I was surprised when I looked back and saw how big the mountain actually was. On the way up all I had seen was the path at my feet and the next few steps to come.

In Rockhampton, Australia, just before my third Olympic Games, I held a press conference. "I love rowing," I said, fighting back tears. "It's always been fun for me. It's always been a challenge, a dream, a game. The Olympics to me are about pushing myself to my limits, testing my preparation and my abilities." I was announcing my withdrawal from the 2000 Sydney Olympics; those Games were finished for me before they even began.

In August 2000, I had flown to the other side of the world with the rest of the Canadian rowing team for our final preparation camp. My body was sore, but I thought my aches and pains were just a normal part of aging. It turned out to be more—way more.

The day after arriving I went for a row. I wasn't two kilometres from the dock when a wave of pain, unlike anything

I'd ever felt, came through me. This wasn't good, and I knew that I'd better turn my boat and head back to the dock. I took a few strokes toward the dock. A tsunami of pain came over me. It was all I could do to remember to breathe as my mind and body began a frantic search for an escape from the pain. A single is about twenty-seven feet long and no more than one foot wide. You are perched more on it than in it. Balance in a single is precarious. There was no escape.

When Al came by in his coach boat, I couldn't speak. He waited for me to explain why I was stopped. "I can't row" was all I could say. I needed him to rescue me because, for the first time in my life, I couldn't help myself at all.

My Olympic races would begin in only three weeks. I couldn't afford a big problem. I refused to believe that Karen (Krash) Orlando, our team physio, whom I had trusted for over five years, could be right when she deduced that it was a disc problem. We quickly got an appointment with an Australian doctor, who instantly agreed with Krash. He made an appointment for me to have an MRI to confirm the diagnosis.

An MRI is an amazing thing. I was put on a table and drawn into the confining cylindrical space. I was alone in the room as the machine around me went through a series of extremely loud knocking and thumping sounds. I was told that I would have to be still for about forty minutes, so to pass the time I went through a stroke-by-stroke mental imagery session that included my warm-up and my Olympic race plan. If I was being kept physically off the water for a few days, I could still prepare in my mind. As always, I made the situation in my mind as challenging as possible. (As if I needed to add more challenge!) In those forty minutes I was still going to the Olympics, and I was going to be the champion.

As I left the MRI lab I turned to the technician. I had no idea how this machine worked. I asked her if the results get sent somewhere to be developed or if she could see them already. She looked at me and said, "Mate, you're going to have to talk to someone who gets paid a lot more than me to tell you that you have a doozie there."

The next day, an image of my vertebrae and spinal column was displayed on a light box as I entered the doctor's office. Even to an untrained eye it was clear. Two discs were clearly shoving my spinal column dramatically out of alignment. We would later determine that one of the discs had actually ruptured; "the jelly had left the doughnut." The doctor looked at me and asked, "Do you want the bad news or the really bad news?"

The bad news was I had two severely prolapsed discs. The really bad news was that this was not a situation that would be fixed in three weeks. Just like that, this Olympic dream was done. Krash drove me in silence to the pharmacy to have my pain prescription filled. I was trying to absorb the news that my Olympic career was over; I was absolutely devastated. It felt like the end of the world to me.

As we walked from the car to the pharmacy, we checked our stride so that a gentleman could go by us on the sidewalk in his wheelchair. In the shop we looked at each other; we were thinking the same thing. Although what was happening to me was pretty bad, it could be way worse. My Olympics may have been over because of a bad back, but I was still able to walk. It was a profound moment of perspective. Sport may have been my passion, but this temporarily broken body of mine was my life.

Our own perspective on our goals, and on the work and the preparation that we do, is always just that: our perspective from our position. Sometimes as we get closer to something, we get tunnel vision and stop seeing it for what it really is. In the same way that we take a moment, like a gopher, to stick our head up and check that we are still digging toward our goal, we need to consciously use that moment to step back and look not just at where we are going but at what we are doing and why, to gain a broader perspective. Our goals are always important, but sometimes we need to check whether there is anything else that is more important.

IF YOU LET THEM
The support team that surrounds you can be an almost limitless source of aid. They can help with the broad perspective as much as with the little details. Some people are very good at allowing others to contribute to their performance. They encourage collaboration and involvement from the variety of people around them and their resources. Others aren't so good at inclusion, but like everything else, it is a skill that you can learn. And like every lesson, it always sinks in a little more when you understand why.

When my disc ruptured in Australia, I struggled to accept that my body had let me down. With the man in the wheelchair in mind, I realized how much we take our mobility for granted. Just getting out of bed in the morning to freshen up or grab some breakfast would result in hours of breath-catching pain.

I was still surrounded by teammates who were the epitome of strength and capability. They were just days away from competing at the Olympics, and I couldn't do anything. I had always been a co-operative team player, but for my own needs, I had tended to take care of everything myself. I enjoyed helping others but was uncomfortable letting others help me. I have to admit that I thought I was uniquely capable of doing my job and helping those around me. This ruptured disc had stripped my independence from me.

One morning when I was getting some breakfast I dropped my fork. I was devastated because I couldn't pick it up. I could hardly touch my knees, let alone reach down to the floor. I had never accepted much help from the people around me, mostly because I had never asked for it. With my back so badly damaged, I had no choice but to ask one of my teammates to help me out. I had never felt so trapped and helpless.

I needed daily physio, massage, and acupuncture to help me manage the pain that continued to swell. A decision was made that I would travel with the team to Sydney so that I could receive treatment to bring the swelling down (which would have to occur before I could fly home) and so that I could watch the Olympic rowing regatta. It had been my dream for so long, I couldn't imagine not being there with, and for, my team.

Sometimes it is hard to get out of the way, especially if you are used to being part of the process. You want to be close and helpful, to share your experience and knowledge. Unconsciously (selfishly?) you may want others to acknowledge you and make you feel essential, important, or at the very least missed. You may very well be essential or important, but sometimes it is in different ways than you think. Suddenly on the outside looking in, I was struck by how incredibly focussed and driven everyone was. They were going to be fine without me.

I chose to be as positive and upbeat around the other rowers as possible. If I moped around the team and looked for their sympathy, it could draw them into my disappointment.

From my perspective, the Olympics were over, but from theirs, they were just about to begin. I wanted them to keep their positive momentum going into competition. Even as broken as I was, it was easier for me to give to my team than to take; I still had so much to learn.

Once again, my injury gave me a unique perspective. Instead of reaching for more myself, I had to let other people do more for me. The day before the team was scheduled to pack up and leave the training camp in Rockhampton for the Olympic Village in Sydney, Henry Hering, one of my teammates, came to my room. Anticipating that I would have to get my luggage down to the lobby the next day, he offered to help. He said that he would come for my bags and ensure that they got loaded on the truck.

It sounds so simple. I'm not sure why it stood out for me then, but I hope it always will. For a very strong athletic person, carrying a piece of luggage isn't a difficult thing. Normally I would never have accepted help for something I could so easily do myself. Henry had gone out of his way to anticipate my need and offer his help, and he sincerely meant it. It may have been a first for me—I accepted help without a struggle. I thanked him and just said yes. For the first time I realized how kind people can be—if you let them.

When I withdrew from the Olympics, I concluded my press conference by saying, "I think everybody has something they're exceptional at, and not everyone is lucky enough to find it. Every day I think I was lucky to find rowing, and I don't want this injury to take that away from me."

The injury took away my goal of competing in the single at the Olympics, but it gave me something too. The injury taught me to use the support around me. I can use my support system to help me train, to help me perform, and even to discover what my next goal could be. People around us have so much to give—if you let them.

When you come home from work, sport, school, or whatever it is that fills your day, the people you come home to are rarely experts or even informed about the details of what you have done all day. To help you, they don't have to be. When you have problems or struggle either physically or mentally, it's too easy to think that they won't understand or can't provide assistance. Unique points of view and debate bring "outside the box" thinking. Letting others be involved and help in their own way encourages flexibility, and more importantly it fosters learning. Being independent is a strength for only so long; eventually being a silo becomes a liability.

NEXT

There are many reasons why you might want to select a new goal to focus on. Whether a result feels like a success, a failure, or neither, once a goal ceases to motivate you, it's time to change. There is no joy in pursuing anything that means nothing to you; you must maintain some desire to apply ambition. It can be very depressing to stick with a goal only because other people expect you to. If you can't connect to any motivation, staying accountable and committed to the goal may become even more difficult.

Accepting that you have reached the end of a goal, even one that you have achieved, can be difficult because you have taught yourself that there is still more. But there *will* always be more. Having arrived at the final photo in your goal-setting photo album, you can create more images to follow. Achieving your goal presents you with the next corridor of doors.

Knowing you want something, but not knowing what that something is, can be very uncomfortable. The absence of a goal does not mean you are without ambition. It just means you haven't found what you want to focus on next. It may be that instead of one large goal, your ambition will get spread among many diverse goals. The combinations and possibilities truly are endless.

Shifting from one goal to the next doesn't always happen quickly. You aren't always given the luxury of knowing what your next goal will be. Retirement in sport, as in business, can be carefully planned or premature. Relocating, changing directions, or changing careers can present the most formidable "Can I? Will I?" moments. Shifting from one major goal to another requires complete buy-in to embrace the value of change and challenge.

Selecting a new goal and applying your ambition to it can be exciting, but remember: if you start at the beginning, let yourself be at the beginning. On a first date you should wonder whether your companion is someone you will enjoy dinner with, not whether he or she is the person you will retire with! Rowing became a huge part of my life, but I didn't expect that on the day I signed up for learn-to-row. If, over time, you have lost yourself in your last goal, you can forget that you are capable of doing something different. It's hard to remember that what became your big passion goal may not have started that way.

Who you were and what you did does not define what you'll do today or tomorrow. You are not your goals or your achievements. They exist because of your ambition; you are so much more. Even so, shifting from one goal to another can be scary. Being open to learning and allowing lessons to come from everywhere are the ultimate tools of a career champion.

Becoming excellent at something is like living in a dream house and figuring out the neighbourhood you live in. You learn where all the best and most convenient shops are, the best traffic routes in and out, which neighbours are helpful and which aren't, and what all of the secret little nooks and crannies are that give an area a special yet familiar character. After a while, though, maybe it's not a great house for you anymore; you grow up and your needs change. It's important to remember that it became a great house and a great neighbourhood because, through exploring and learning, you made it that way. A champion has the skills to do that again, somewhere new.

Sometimes you will have to start, or restart, at the very beginning, in a whole new house, in a whole new neighbourhood. Your ego may not be keen to start on the ground floor again. It may be true that mighty oaks grow from tiny acorns and a trip of a thousand miles begins with one step, but not everyone wants to start at square one. This is easy enough for the young and blissfully naive but can be off-putting to those who have followed the path and know the challenges that may come. Having done it at least once should lead us to be confident that we can do it again, but often experience just makes us remember how hard it was starting up. This is a bit of a mistake, because a large part of what made it hard the first time was that we lacked the skills that we now take for granted.

It is a mistake to think that restarting with a mostly empty cup is the same as starting at the beginning. Because of our life experiences, some grains of rice will return very quickly. But if you think you are above a little hard work and getting your hands a bit dirty, you are unlikely to venture toward change. Arrogance and entitlement can interfere with accepting new goals that may seem beneath you. Your next challenge—be it building your dream house in a new neighbourhood, changing careers, or picking a new hobby—will remain a simple dream or idea. When you are ready to absorb it, anticipating some change and challenge can lead to something new and exciting.

NORMAL PEOPLE

In 2005, the Canadian Olympic Team hosted a conference for athletes and coaches preparing for the 2006 Winter Olympics in Turin. I was asked to be the closing keynote speaker for the Olympic Excellence Series. I had been speaking to corporate groups for over ten years on motivation, focus, and belief in big goals. I was confident that I could address this group without any problem. My presentation spoke about the normalcy of the Olympic journey. Yes, it was an extreme form of living, but it was also something that normal people, like me, can do.

I based my presentation on normal people doing special things. I really wanted to bring home that Olympic champions had all of the same fears and doubts that other people did. To find success at the Olympics, to become a champion yourself, you first have to recognize that champions are normal people.

Later that day, when I was in the airport lounge waiting to fly home, some of the athletes who had been at the event approached me. "You don't *really* see yourself as normal, do you?" they asked. "You have three gold medals!" "Absolutely," I said. At that moment another corridor of doors presented itself to me. The sign on this one was Mentor.

I was curious, and I wanted to try. I was prepared to be their mentor. If nothing else, I could help them embrace the idea that being normal doesn't exclude them from doing incredible things; everyone is normal. Heck, if I could do it,

I was quite sure that they could! I understand that there is a unique culture to each sport; I had a lot to learn, but I could try to help as I was learning.

Eleven of the fourteen sport groups that heard my presentation requested that I do follow-up talks in their training camps later that year. The Canadian Olympic Committee also wanted to include my message in a new program that it was developing.

Making a national team is hard and stressful, but making an Olympic team and then qualifying for the Olympics is exponentially more so. The Olympics are different because the performance may be the same routine, but it means way more. I've seen an athlete who was a three-time world champion fret about her ability to become an Olympic champion. She worried that she might not be deserving! She was having a tough time connecting her normal self to her dream of winning at the Olympics. The grand scale of everything that happens at the Olympics makes them an awesome experience, but a bigger reason why they are so special, I believe, is that more people care.

The COC's athlete preparation program was developed to help athletes cope with the particular issues that arise not just from the seventeen days of the Olympics but also from the months and years that precede the Games. A lot of work is similar to that. It's not just the actual test that is deeply stressful; being selected to do the job, preparation for the test, and anticipation of it also weigh on us.

Although there is a tremendous amount of external pressure on an athlete who is preparing for the Olympics, the very fact that the Olympics have been a lifelong dream multiplies the internal pressure. The Olympics are unique, but the stress isn't much different from what most people experience. Almost everyone puts more pressure on themselves than other people do; we care and worry about our own performance and results more than anyone else.

Before the 2006 Turin Olympics, the preparation program brought a small group of athletes to an Olympic Excellence Series conference or two. Then the program broadened its reach to include visits to training camps from Olympic mentors like me. Before the 2010 Vancouver Olympics, the program added another significant feature: professional development/mentor messages were sent regularly to every-one—athletes, coaches, and their support teams—preparing for the Games. The goal of these messages was to help them cope with the variety of emotions, like doubts, fears, and pride, that would accompany them on their journey. We wanted Canadian athletes to arrive at the Olympics with all of the ego and confidence that they had worked so hard to attain. We wanted the Canadian team to keep their swagger.

As the athletes travelled the world to train, compete, and qualify for the 2010 Winter Olympics, in my role as mentor, I wrote simple messages that tried to normalize the quest to achieve a massive goal—and the grandness of the Olympic lifestyle. I got some great replies, in which the athletes said they now recognized that it was okay to feel powerful and it was so good not to feel alone anymore.

That, I discovered, is the secret to performance. Knowing that you're not alone in how you feel is amazingly powerful. People want to know that their thoughts, whether they are confident or doubtful, aren't wrong. That reassurance (which does not need to include confirmation that you are right— just that you are not wrong) is what allows you to have the audacity to reach for more. As you approach the "Can I? Will I?" moments that immediately precede the object of your desire, you just want to know that you aren't crazy for trying. Being scared does not mean that you aren't a champion. Experienced champions are comfortable with their fears and their confidence; these become familiar ingredients in every win.

SUCCESS OR CONFIDENCE

I was once asked to do a presentation on success and confidence, and I began to wonder whether this is a chicken-and-egg conundrum. Which comes first, success or confidence? Do you need to be successful to be confident? Or do you need to be confident to be successful?

People define success differently and are ambitious for different reasons. Confidence can present itself very differently from person to person. Some people are more comfortable being confident than others, just as some embrace success more easily. Is that nature or nurture? It's hard to know.

Often young athletes start off blissfully naive. They just don't have the experience to know that what they are doing is considered hard or dangerous. Without having experienced any success, they are still boldly confident. They do what they have been training to do, and they see no reason not to be confident.

I have seen people become confident, and more comfortable being confident, as they experience success. I've also seen highly successful people struggle with being confident.

When Anne Montminy, a Canadian diver, was preparing for the 1996 Olympic Games, she was told repeatedly that the way to win was through positive imagery and self-belief. Ranked in the top five in the world, Anne adopted this advice even though it was contrary to what had previously worked for her. She struggled with it; positive, self-confident thinking did nothing but make her feel uncomfortable. She underperformed and told me she felt embarrassed when she failed to finish in the top twenty at the Atlanta Olympics.

For the next four years, as she prepared for the Sydney Olympics, she returned to using the techniques that had made her successful before Atlanta. Anne was more comfortable thinking that she was the worst competitor in the field and that she was always on the verge of making a huge mistake. It worked for her; she won silver and bronze Olympic medals. Anne did not need to be confident to be successful, but she did need to be prepared.

Confidence and success are the results of preparation. You don't have to have confidence to have success, nor do you have to have success to have confidence. Preparation determines the quality of all of our performances. You don't always know what you are preparing for, but if you are learning, you are always putting grains of rice into your cup—and there is a value to every grain of rice.

Creative thinking allows a lesson learned on one goal-achieving path to be applied to the next. Grains of rice are transferable. When I was young I played quite a bit of chess. Like most things I do, I got competitive at it, played in tournaments, and achieved a top-twenty-five national ranking for kids under twelve. It's wrong to think that once I left competitive chess, I left that world behind. I continue to use lessons I learned from chess every day. Thinking many moves ahead and considering my offensive and defensive options is a life skill. The strategy and tactics that I learned through chess were grains of rice in my cup that contributed to my winning Olympic gold medals in rowing.

BEST FEELING EVER

The Vancouver 2010 Olympics were even more special than other Olympics. They were a home Games; Canada was the host nation. For the previous two years, all of the talk and theory had been about the extra pressure and expectations that would be placed on the team when they would compete in front of a home crowd. In fact, it turned out to be quite the opposite. As the Olympic Torch Relay made its way from the east coast to the west, Canadians wanted to give nothing but their enthusiastic support and love. The athletes were happy to take it.

The Canadian team settled into the village. The "My Team Is..." posters that the team members had created with the five words that represented them hung throughout their residential space. Those words—*confident, ready, passionate, resilient,* and *united*—were used as art to decorate the walls around them. As they arrived in Vancouver, you could sense that they believed those words.

As February 12, 2010, the day of the Opening Ceremony, approached, the atmosphere in the Olympic Village was electrifying. The 5,500 athletes and officials from around the world all knew that in the next seventeen days they would be faced with their ultimate "Can I? Will I?" moments. Before any Olympics begin, all athletes believe that they will attack and that their dreams can come true; the intensity of hope and confidence was palpable.

In my support role, I was part of a very small group who would march into the Opening Ceremony as support for the athletes. It would be the fifth time that I'd marched with a Canadian Olympic Team. I'd been to three as an athlete, and Vancouver was my second as support staff. In Beijing, I'd had this same herding role, and I joked that I had been the team's border collie. I walked at the back and gently corralled everyone forward as a group. In Vancouver, being the Canadian at the very back meant that I would be the last person to enter the stadium.

As host nation, Canada would be the last of the eighty countries marching in. It is an honour and very exciting for any country to come last, but it also meant that we would have to wait for over five thousand people to march in before us. Sometimes I feel that the Olympic motto, *"Citius, Altius, Fortius,"* could be replaced by "Hurry up and wait." Over 250 Canadians were all dressed up and ready to go. On a warm Vancouver evening, in our Team Canada sweaters, jackets, toques, and scarves, we walked what seemed to be laps of the B.C. Place stadium.

The route we followed went underneath the stands and through the guts of the stadium. We could hear the crowd cheering as the other countries marched in, but since we were at the back of that long line we couldn't see much at all. All I could see was the Canadian team stretched out in front of me as it moved slowly through the grey cement tunnel. Soon enough it would be all bright lights and colours—but until then it was a confining echo chamber of just us.

And then it happened.

From the back, all I saw was our flag making a turn to the left. Clara Hughes led the team up a ramp; at its apex she would then lead the Canadian Olympic Team down another ramp and into the Opening Ceremony. Fifty-five thousand Canadians were waiting to roar. It felt as if we had been marching along aimlessly for over an hour, but suddenly the pace and the energy of the team were different.

What I saw will stay with me as my favourite moment of those Games. I enjoyed it so much I actually skipped and jumped for joy. Behind Clara, the Canadians marched up that ramp with supreme swagger! Their confidence and passion oozed from them. They were a team united by their goals. As they marched up and into that stadium, I was overcome with pride. While I take no credit for any of the incredible performances that were to come, I had been a small part of their preparation. *They were so ready.*

The Canadian athletes were ready to break Olympic records with their success. Their preparation was unparalleled. No other country has ever won so many gold medals at the Winter Games. They were extraordinary yet absolutely normal Canadians, who were ready to do something wonderful. It's an incredible thing to see, and it reminded me that it's an incredible thing to feel: to be ready.

All of the work, the endless, relentless pursuit for more, is absolutely worth it. Your ambition is the key. It gets you started on turning your dreams into goals and encourages you to accept some stress in your lives and be not quite satisfied with your status quo. Your ambition is what motivates you to do all of the hard work and preparation that your goals and curiosity lead you to. Reaching for big, even infinite goals will always be a bit scary. Achieving those goals, having confidence and success, becomes more and more possible with each little +1 more.

∞+1

INDEX